From Layoff to Take-Off: 31 Practical Concepts to Make a Meaningful Transition After a Layoff

Sanjay Patel

Published by Sanjay Patel, 2024.

While every precaution has been taken in the preparation of this book, the publisher assumes no responsibility for errors or omissions, or for damages resulting from the use of the information contained herein.

FROM LAYOFF TO TAKE-OFF: 31 PRACTICAL CONCEPTS TO MAKE A MEANINGFUL TRANSITION AFTER A LAYOFF

First edition. January 24, 2024.

Copyright © 2024 Sanjay Patel.

ISBN: 979-8224757374

Written by Sanjay Patel.

Table of Contents

From Layoff to Take-Off
31 Practical Concepts to Make a Meaningful Transition after a Layoff
By Sanjay J. Patel

Acknowledgments

I have many people to thank for their generosity and willingness to read and critique every word of this new and revised book. I am forever grateful to them. A special thanks to my family and dear friends for their time and endless wisdom regarding my authorship journey.

Introduction

This book is not "the answer" to every life disruption like divorce, serious illness, or death. Rather, this book addresses a disruption in the work life journey – the layoff. The practical concepts presented here are ideas you can apply today to make a successful transition in the aftermath of a layoff. My inspiration for this book is to get you started on the path to pursuing the next chapter of your work life journey – one filled with clear thought, renewed passion, more joy, and greater success. There are no guarantees in life. Therefore, we must learn from the past, embrace the present and prepare for the future.

"Prepare for your future, for that is where you will spend the rest of your life."
Mark Twain

Since the dawn of the United States economy, we have experienced times of tremendous economic growth, painful recession, and financially paralyzing depression. The economy remains a complex phenomenon, which offers no guarantees for anyone or any organization. Rather, the economy presents only one certainty: volatility – both good and bad. This volatility is the result of a myriad of factors, many of which are simply beyond the comprehension of the average American – like me!

In the aftermath of the "great recession," in 2008/2009, many people continue to face financial hardship and adversity from one the worst time periods in the history of the United States. This book confronts the life-changing events affecting so many people, from entry level to middle management, at one time or another. This life-changing event is a workforce reduction, which is corporate language for a layoff. Millions of people, from all backgrounds, lost their jobs during one of the worst economic climates since the Great Depression.

As history has shown, the economy eventually stabilized and actually entered a period of tremendous growth and expansion for several years leading up to the next worldwide event, which sent the global economy on the brink of colossal economic/financial and human catastrophe – the global pandemic. The complexity, uncertainty, and many other dynamics of the global economy continue to evolve. Meanwhile, the last "great recession" and recent pandemic cut far and deep into corporate payrolls, individual savings, and retirement accounts. All sectors of the international marketplace were adversely impacted – operationally and financially – by the global economic downturn. Millions around the world are desperate to pick up the pieces of shattered hopes and dreams and recapture some small sense of normalcy.

People from all backgrounds are confronting the far-reaching implications of the weakened economic environment. Everyone from students, farmers and entrepreneurs to entry-level workers and middle managers continue to face widespread uncertainty about the future of the American economy and global marketplace. While experience, skills, and knowledge are important, they offer no guarantees to overcome a layoff. Today, you need to think "outside the box" to move forward from a layoff. Employers are no longer focusing just on what you know. Rather, employers want to know how you can add value or make a difference to consider you as a viable job candidate.

When revenues and profits continue to decline in a financial sector laden with widespread risk and uncertainty. As a result, many organizations initiate workforce reduction programs, implement pay cuts, and require mandatory unpaid furlough days. On one side, the layoff presents an abrupt and unwelcome result of corporate distress. On the other side, believe it or not, the layoff may offer an opportunity to discover a new direction in your work life journey.

As you read this book, today's news is history and new developments are evolving to shape the future. Over the course of my professional journey, I was fortunate to collaborate with some talented and successful people in the business world. However, I have also experienced the emptiness of losing my job on more than one occasion. Many people worldwide have encountered a similar fate – some of whom have only been with one organization for their entire lives. These are real people, like you and me, from all walks of life, just trying to do the best they can for themselves and the ones they love.

This book presents a glimpse into the chaotic business world as seen through the eyes of characters who, like you, are ordinary people trying to deal with real work life challenges. The situations the characters in this book experience may differ from what you have experienced. And what the characters know and understand may vary from what you know and understand. However, the one thing you have in common is a desire to achieve success and experience joy throughout the work life journey.

This book is divided into three sections – Reaction, Reflection, and Renewal – which represent the three phases of what I call the "emotional and psychological migration." The Reaction section explores the immediate and emotionally turbulent impact of a layoff. The Reflection section discusses the time, commitment, and effort necessary to overcome the layoff. Finally, the Renewal section provides inspiration to put you on the path to recovery from the layoff.

This book shares practical concepts and ideas designed to help bring deeper meaning to the pursuit of finding the next job in the aftermath of a layoff. In addition, there are numerous "personal challenges" throughout the book to help you apply the practical concepts discussed. These probing questions and activities are designed to kick-start your thought process and take action. Your commitment to complete the personal challenges can enhance your ability to overcome the layoff and make a transition into a new opportunity in the work life journey.

Over the course of our lives, we encounter life-changing moments, which can offer unbelievable joy or unwanted sorrow. I do not know about you, but for me, life is a gigantic roller-coaster ride moving forward from one peak to the next valley on a daily basis – or so it seems. The work life journey, or work life roller coaster, is unique for everyone. You need to develop the ability to adapt to changing times, conditions, and priorities to dictate the path, speed, and future direction of your work life journey. Of course, this is easier said than done.

They say actions speak louder than words, which certainly applies to the concepts discussed in this book. You can only control what you think, believe, do, and say. It is my hope this book offers a thought, idea, or concept to help address your current situation. The concepts apply regardless of whether you have a job or are looking for the next bountiful opportunity in your work life journey.

It does not matter what your industry or vocation is; it does not matter whether you seek a white-collar or blue-collar job; it does not matter whether you are currently employed; it does not matter that you might be self-employed; and it does not matter what your career level is. Regardless of your circumstance, this book offers guidance to make your job search after a layoff, or continuation of your current work life journey, more fulfilling.

As you read this book, I encourage you to take a journey through the minds of the characters portrayed and the concepts discussed. They represent the spirit of making the meaningful transition from "Layoff to Take-off" – rising to the challenge to continue the work life journey.

Dedication

This work is dedicated to my loving wife, Manisha, and our three beautiful children - Aavik, Anjali, and Aashay. You are the inspiration of my life and the reason I believe in tomorrow. To my mom, dad, sister, brother-in-law, and two adorable nieces – your love, guidance, and wisdom have filled my life with eternal joy and happiness.

Reaction

"Life is 10% of what happens to me and 90% of how I react to it."
John Maxwell

Beginning of the End

Monday, December 22nd – the entire office is festive, decorated in the spirit of the holiday season. Red and green streamers are strung across the ceiling, while the white and green Christmas trees scatter throughout the office glisten in a cascade of colorful lights. Holiday cards are on display in the break room; festive wreathes hang on office doors; and floral arrangements are on the conference room tables. Images of holiday cheer appear everywhere.

Yet, the office is almost empty. Many staff members are taking these precious days leading up to the Christmas Eve and Christmas Day holidays to spend time with family and friends. Meanwhile, the office management team is gathering to make some critical and tough decisions in preparation for the beginning of the new fiscal year. It is not a joyous time for management.

The company, due to current global economic conditions, is experiencing its seventh consecutive quarter of declining financial results. In fact, this fiscal year-end will result in the first annual net loss in the 18-year history of the company. During that time, turnover has been relatively low compared to other companies in the same market. Since personnel changes are so infrequent, the entire management team is uneasy and concerned about the tough decisions being finalized and the future impact of such decisions.

John, the president and CEO of the company, lives by four fundamental principles: focus on the customer, accountability across all personnel, a healthy corporate culture, and a strong commitment to the future. However, today those principles are being challenged unlike ever before because one-third of the company workforce will be impacted by the first employee layoff in the history of the organization.

Soon, 200 employees will be laid off from the organization. A once-proud company with 600 employees will be a much smaller firm with only 400. Among those being let go, two people in particular are especially difficult for John, as they were among the first to join him at the start of the company. While the layoff news is upsetting for many, not everyone receives the bad news in the same manner.

Those who know John understand he is a people person, and that loyalty has always been very important to him. To compound matters, the company is making these layoff decisions during the holiday season, when joy and happiness should fill the air of homes and offices worldwide.

Dark Monday

Monday, January 5th, 10 AM – Bob, an accounting supervisor, receives a message to go see his boss Mark, the controller. Bob quickly realizes this individual meeting is unusual, because meetings are announced during the prior week. However, there is no announcement for a team meeting today, so Bob starts to wonder about the meeting with his boss.

Bob, like most people in the company, is aware of current economic conditions and the overall state of the company. Revenue and profits are declining sharply. As a result, Bob knows company sales managers and account representatives come and go. However, operational functions such as Accounting, Human Resources, and Accounts Payable are more stable.

Bob heads down the pathway near the second-floor windows overlooking the large forest preserve at the back of the office complex. He is nervous as he walks by several office cubicles on his way to the corner office, which belongs to his boss, Mark. As Bob enters Mark's office, he sees the elegant cherry mahogany desk and bookshelves adorned with several family pictures. A subdued voice greets Bob. "Hi Bob, please have a seat. Bob, this is Jennifer, from our Human Resources Department, and she is going to talk to you about a difficult subject," Mark explains as calmly as he can.

Jennifer shakes Bob's hand and begins to talk about the meeting. "Bob, by now, I am sure you are aware of the adverse impact the economy has had on the company for over a year. As a result, the senior management team decided to eliminate some positions in the company. Your position is one that has been eliminated," Jennifer states in a sincere manner.

After Jennifer explains the purpose of the meeting, Mark informs Bob, "We want you to know this decision had absolutely nothing to do with your performance." At this point, Bob appears numb and somewhat shocked, as he looks down and begins to shake his head in disbelief. Jennifer continues, "That's right Bob. The decision to eliminate your position was not based on anything you did wrong. Rather, there were many factors that contributed to the workforce reduction program being executed in several areas and locations of the company."

After a few moments of silence, Jennifer begins to discuss the severance package the company has prepared for Bob. "Given your lengthy and exemplary service to the company, we want to offer you a severance package. We believe this package will offer you and your family some comfort during this difficult and challenging time," Jennifer says in a sincere tone. "I realize this meeting may raise many questions and emotions, so we want to provide as much as assistance as possible to help you through this process," Jennifer says.

———●———

In addition to the severance amount, the company also will cover a portion of the monthly medical, dental and vision premium costs, should Bob choose to select such coverage. The company also offers Bob a three-month membership with a local organization specializing in outplacement services. Finally, the company will provide use of the employee assistance program for help in dealing with the emotional and psychological impact of the layoff.

Bob joined the company after graduating from college. He represents the rare example of an employee who has experienced the many ups and downs of the company from the beginning. Bob is a dedicated employee with a passion for quality work, a strong focus on details and accuracy, and respect for his colleagues.

Bob has been recognized as employee of the month several times and been promoted twice during his tenure with the company. He is the typical white-collar professional living in a suburb of Chicago with his wife, Mary, and their two delightful children - Michael, nine, and Sarah, six - and Ruffles, the family dog. With an outstanding employment history and record of achievement, Bob has enjoyed a successful career thus far.

Given his history with the company, Bob struggles to make sense of the layoff and wonders why it is happening to him. Bob begins to think about his long history with the company. He has experienced good and bad times within the company, but nothing quite like this.

⸺⚬⸺

Monday, January 5th, 10 AM – Sally, a customer service manager, receives a message to see her boss, David, at 11 a.m. This meeting request is like so many of the other meeting requests she has had for the past several years. However today, Sally is also feeling somewhat concerned as news of layoffs at other companies is being announced on a daily basis.

Sally meets David and Judy, a Human Resources representative, in the conference room adjacent to the main elevators. Sally is noticeably nervous and overwhelmed by what she believes is the reason for the meeting – she thinks she is going to be laid off.

At this point, David begins the meeting with some brief words. "Sally, I have some bad news; it is with deep regret I inform you your position within the company has been eliminated. However, at no time was your performance a reason behind this action," explains David. "In fact, you exemplify what quality customer service means," David emphasizes time and again during the meeting.

"I want you to know this was a very difficult decision for me and the entire management team. Good people like you are hard to find, and so I assure you this is the last thing we ever wanted to do," David says as sincerely as possible. Sally's first reaction to the news is utter disappointment and disbelief. She struggles to control her emotions as tears begin to run down her face. Visibly upset, Sally tries to regain control and begin to somehow rationalize what she has just heard. At first, she says nothing, continuing to listen patiently and wait until she can gather her strength and find the right words to maintain her dignity.

However, David and Judy are just as distraught as Sally. This layoff decision has by no means been easy for them. David, in particular, is having some difficulty controlling his emotions – for he was once laid off. "A layoff is the last thing a company wants to pursue with its best people," David says again. "I believe quality people like you, Sally, make all the difference in the world; however, there are times when an organization experiences extraordinary challenges, which require some very tough decisions.

"In this case, the company is outsourcing the entire Customer Service function to a third-party firm," David continues. By now, Sally composes herself again and begins to think about the immediate future. Judy then chimes in again to discuss the severance package the company has to offer Sally. While the severance package offers some relief, Sally also knows she must prepare for a future beyond the severance. Sally realizes she is fortunate to receive a severance package, given the current state of the economy.

<hr>

Sally joined the company as a customer service representative during its first year of existence; management quickly realized Sally was an absolute natural at providing high-quality customer service. Over the years, Sally demonstrated her knowledge and skill repeatedly. She had been the recipient of the Outstanding Customer Service Award several times. And, Sally had been promoted two times over the course of her career at the company.

Sally's severance package includes access to outplacement services and a monthly subsidy for health benefits. In addition, she has access to the employee assistance program for emotional and psychological stress from the layoff. Although Sally is pleased to learn about the details of the severance package, she is also concerned about the when, what, and why questions behind her being laid off.

Sally is a single mother raising a bright 15-year-old daughter named Ashley. Sally has a challenging life. She is not a college graduate, although she is not far from earning an undergraduate degree in business management. Sally needs only six more courses to complete her degree. Unfortunately, her husband, Barry, died after a lengthy battle with cancer soon after Ashley was born. Since then, Sally's sole focus in life has been her daughter.

The days and weeks turned into months and years, and Sally never went back to school to complete her degree. Sally's personality, ability to learn quickly, commitment to quality, and respect for others are her greatest personal attributes. Many of her customers commented on those attributes several times during Sally's tenure with the company.

Given her length of service, Sally is finding it difficult to understand why she is being laid off after such a successful career with the company. It will take some time for Sally to fully grasp the impact of the layoff.

⎯⎯⎯◉⎯⎯⎯

Monday, January 5th, 4 PM – For Vince, a senior assembler at the manufacturing plant located in South Carolina, the layoff news is anything but sensible or respectful. He is laid off after a full day at work without any face-to-face interaction with his boss Robert, the plant manager. In fact, Vince learns of his fate when he clocks out for the day shift and returns to his locker. Today does not seem different from any other workday over the past 17 years. As Vince approaches his locker, he notices a small white envelope with his name on it.

Vince opens the envelope to find a typed note stating the following: "Due to budget cuts, the corporate office is eliminating 25 jobs at this manufacturing plant. Your position is among the jobs being eliminated, effective immediately. We thank you for your service to this organization over the years and wish your luck in your future employment endeavors."

There was no signature on the note, just "Plant Management" typed in plain text "'Plant Management!'" Vince yells. "What the hell is this? Unbelievable! Nothing but a plain note with cold language directed to an employee who gave 17 years of his life to this company." Vince is overwhelmed with anger as he punches his locker, kicks the wooden bench behind him, and throws his water bottle in rage.

After reading the note, Vince storms into his manager's office. However, Robert is nowhere to be found, having left earlier in the day on a personal matter. While Vince is overcome with anger and emptiness, he quickly realizes he too needs to just get away from the plant. Without further delay, he grabs his personal belongings and walks toward the front door and out into the parking lot.

As Vince leaves the building, a soft tapping on his shoulder stops him in his tracks. Charlene, the office clerk, appears behind Vince wanting to say goodbye to a long-time colleague and friend. "Vince, I am so sorry about today," she says as her eyes fill with tears. "It just won't be the same without you here. I never thought such a day would come for this company," she says, her voice almost cracking on every word. Vince still feels rage rushing through his body, yet manages to comfort Charlene by giving her a goodbye hug. Their friendship will continue even though his employment with the company is over.

Meanwhile, Vince has more serious concerns to address regarding his immediate future. He has a wife, Susan, and a 7-year-old son, Dillon, to support. Fortunately, Susan still has her receptionist job. However, her income is hardly enough to support the family. Vince is noticeably worried and wonders how he and his family will get through the financial crisis ahead.

———◦———

At 41, Vince is beyond the young, energetic person he was when he first joined the company. Vince never went to college and life has been a constant challenge. When Vince was just four years old, his father abandoned him and his mother. Vince was raised by his mom, who died shortly after Vince graduated high school.

Vince lived with relatives for awhile, but eventually returned to his hometown and pursued odd jobs for the next seven years. Then, at 24, Vince landed a job at a local manufacturing plant, which proved to be the starting point of a 17-year employment history with one employer. During that time, Vince decided not to pursue any further education, as he was content with the job and never paid much attention to the notion of a "career."

In addition to lost income, Vince and his family are facing a future with no health benefits. Market health coverage is not an option because it is just too expensive. And, there are many bills to pay – the mortgage, the car, monthly utilities, and the three-month-old flat-panel, 50-inch, high-definition LED television.

The only good news on an otherwise dreadful day is Vince has set aside a modest amount of savings over the years. But, this is enough to sustain his family for nine months. Although Vince will pursue unemployment benefits, he knows a more secure future is necessary to support his family and hopefully plan for some kind of retirement.

So, what is Vince going to do? Where is he going to find another stable job? More importantly, how is going to find another job? Every manufacturer in a 50-mile radius is experiencing financial hardship and announcing layoffs. With no college degree and experience limited to factory work, Vince's options to re-enter the workforce are limited.

Like Bob and Sally, Vince faces some tough questions. While they each come from a different situation in the work life journey, are all enduring the sudden emptiness of a layoff.

Layoff is Not Personal

For Bob, Sally, and Vince, the painful reality of the layoff is truly perplexing. On the one hand, they all had lengthy and successful tenures with the company. On the other hand, their hard work and contributions to the company have vanished with a sudden, life-changing decision impacting their future. It is natural to experience a wide range of thoughts and emotions in a layoff situation.

It is also a normal reaction to seek answers to many questions resulting from a layoff. However, the first hurdle to overcome in a layoff situation is to accept the reality of the layoff. Let me say it again, you need to *accept the reality of the layoff.*

For Bob, Sally, and Vince, the layoff was not a result of poor performance or any other negative actions. Rather, the layoff was due to many factors beyond their control. For example, the state of the economy, lower revenues and profits, market share erosion, and competitive pressures all contributed to a sharp decline in the company's financial performance. As a result, the senior management team decided a workforce reduction was the best course of action to help stabilize the company's operational and financial performance going forward. In addition to layoffs, senior management also decided to freeze merit increases, eliminate bonus payments, and suspend all hiring.

For many, it is too easy to assess personal blame for a layoff. However, layoffs have little to do with job performance. It is the economic climate, changes in organizational strategy, or the financial condition of the company that lead to a workforce reduction. In fact, a workforce reduction is typically the last action taken by an organization seeking to "right the ship" and stop the financial bleeding.

The layoff is an action taken to reduce future personnel costs – often one of the largest line-item expenses on the profit and loss statement.

However, a layoff can also weaken the operational effectiveness of an organization because there are fewer people to perform daily business operations. As a result, the workload is redistributed among the employees not otherwise affected by the workforce reduction. Consequently, a layoff creates an emotional and psychological "ripple effect" impacting everyone – those laid off as well as those who remain on the corporate payroll.

Emotional and Psychological Migration

Bob and Sally met with their bosses and discovered the jobs they had performed for so many years had suddenly been eliminated. And, they had no prior knowledge these life-changing decisions were going to happen. After the shock, the immediate reaction from Bob and Sally was not different. Both were overwhelmed with similar emotions – disappointment, frustration, denial, fear, and sudden emptiness. For John, the CEO, the morning is just as emotional, because Bob and Sally have been with John from the early years of the company.

Soon after the meetings with Bob and Sally, the entire office is buzzing about the developments of the day. Amidst the storm lies a quiet rage only those who have been laid off can truly understand. Both Bob and Sally begin gathering their belongings in preparation for their departure.

As a personable leader, John takes time to meet Bob and Sally individually. "I am so sorry for today," he says, trying to collect his thoughts and speak with a firm tone. "I never imagined we would ever make such difficult decisions, nor can I even begin to understand what you must be thinking or feeling now. For me, I never forget those who have stayed by my side through good times and bad."

Bob and Sally each expressed their sincere gratitude to John for his thoughtful comments. Although they both were overcome with disappointment and sadness, they understand just how difficult the layoff decision was for John as well. While the layoff decision was a painful reality for Bob and Sally, John reassured them by offering some words of encouragement as they left the company.

Vince, on the other hand, did not have the opportunity to speak with plant management regarding his layoff and is facing the aftermath of a layoff alone. With so many thoughts and emotions racing through his mind, Vince has no idea what to do next or what he is going to tell his wife and son.

The ability to overcome the challenge presented by a layoff is largely up to Bob, Sally, and Vince. In other words, when a layoff occurs, you need to first acknowledge or accept the layoff. Only then can you begin managing the spectrum of emotions and thoughts caused by the layoff. **I refer to this process as an emotional and psychological migration – the first practical concept to understand in the aftermath of a layoff.** Table 1 illustrates the three phases of the emotional and psychological migration and some of the common emotional and psychological attributes characterizing each phase.

Table 1 – Emotional and Psychological Migration

Reaction Phase	Reflection Phase	Renewal Phase
Anger	Concern	Anxiety
Denial	Fear	Eagerness
Emptiness	Isolation	Focus
Frustration	Stress	Optimism
Sadness	Uncertainty	Confidence

The reaction phase is the most intense and emotionally explosive phase. People often experience a mixed set of emotions in the immediate aftermath of a layoff. For Bob and Sally, the feelings of fear and sadness were overwhelming. For others, like Vince, anger and frustration were the dominant emotions. Some people may also experience denial or even depression. For me, sadness and fear were the overriding concerns.

No matter what emotions surface after the layoff, the reaction phase typically includes a lot of negative energy. This negative energy can create serious ripple effects if not quickly identified and controlled. The emotional impact of a layoff is hard enough. However, the impact of a layoff on the mind and body can also be quite serious. Health concerns such as depression, anxiety and stress should not be underestimated. It is important to limit the amount of time spent in the reaction phase – one or two days are enough. However, the actual amount of time in the reaction phase is entirely up to you.

Many people visually and verbally express their emotions when the layoff occurs and often continue to do so long after the layoff. For example, it is easy to express anger and frustration verbally as a common reaction to the layoff. However, expressing such negative energy never helps the situation or takes away the painful reality. I am not suggesting you just bottled up your emotions. Rather, you must find a constructive way to release your negative energy. There is a good anonymous quote that offers great wisdom for any layoff situation: "The fact that we are born with two eyes and two ears suggests we ought to look and listen twice as much as we speak." In other words, do not allow your emotions to overrule logic, common sense, and civility, especially in a layoff situation.

Time and effort must be devoted to successfully migrate from the reaction phase to the reflection phase. The reflection phase is where you gain perspective and understanding of not only what has happened, but also what needs to be done next. Therefore, just talking to someone – a colleague, friend or loved one – can offer tremendous help. The simple act of talking can provide much needed emotional and psychological therapy to begin dealing with the layoff.

Just as the reaction phase is unique for anyone who has experienced a layoff, so too is the reflection phase. The reflection phase requires you to carefully reassess your specific situation before you make any further work life journey related decisions and choices. On the same token, the reflection phase also provides an opportunity to evaluate and prioritize your goals and objectives. You also identify your strengths, weaknesses, likes, dislikes, needs, and wants.

For Bob, the reflection phase will involve gaining a deep understanding of his inventory of personal attributes to determine his ideal path for professional progression. For Sally, the reflection phase will provide the opportunity to reassess her technical and educational goals. Bob and Sally also have an opportunity to re-think their career goals, which may reveal opportunities to transition from one industry into another. For Vince, the reflection phase will illuminate the need and opportunity to pursue more knowledge and skills, as well as utilize other talents.

For me, the reflection phase offered the opportunity to rebalance my needs and wants. I have a saying, "I do not want what I cannot have, and I only want what I truly need." Yes, you can call me silly, crazy, or whatever other adjective works for you. In the end, you must take the time and make the effort to overcome your negative energy and focus on more productive ideas and endeavors.

While there is no set time limit for the reflection phase, it is important to allow yourself to fully assess your current situation. You need to think about how you want to continue the work life journey going forward. For this reason, it is realistic to expect the reflection phase to last for several days or few weeks, which should help you prepare adequately for the renewal phase.

The renewal phase is the final phase of the emotional and psychological migration. In the renewal phase, you learn, or discover the desire, to move on. You focus your attention on finding new opportunities to make a fresh start with a new organization. The renewal phase presents the starting point for the job search process. For this reason, the renewal phase is often the longest portion of the emotional and psychological migration.

In the renewal phase, you feel more comfortable talking about the layoff and the challenges of finding a job. You are also more willing to collaborate with others (family, friends, colleagues, recruiters, and others) because the focus is no longer on the layoff. Rather, the focus is on moving forward into new opportunities to continue the work life journey.

It is important to note the emotional and psychological migration is not always a linear progression. In other words, it is quite possible to experience a regression back into the reflection phase or even the reaction phase. While your desire is to move forward, you may find yourself going backward. Remember, there are no guarantees in the job search. You need to stay focused and committed to completing a successful migration.

During the early part of my work life journey, I interviewed with a technology company offering innovative solutions for corporate tax departments. Because I had several years of practical corporate tax experience, I was given the chance to interview for a manager level role within the organization. The idea was to assist existing customers to gain more effective use of the technology, while engaging in activities to position the technology with prospective customers.

The interview process was lengthy, as I met with several staff and management level personnel in the company. After a three-week interviewing process, the hiring manager told me an offer for employment was imminent. In fact, he introduced me to the human resources manager and compensation manager to discuss salary, completion of forms and employee benefits. I was quite excited with the development and looked forward to making a successful transition. Unfortunately, I never got the chance to make a meaningful transition.

The day after I met with the human resources manager, I received a call from the hiring manager. He informed me my "imminent" job offer was no longer a reality. Can you imagine the thoughts racing through my mind? I was confused and caught off guard. I asked the hiring manager why I was no longer a candidate for the job. His reply was a complete surprise to me. The CEO of the company decided I was not the "ideal" candidate for the job because I was not a certified public accountant (CPA). Although I had many other attributes that qualified me for the job, one specific item was the reason why I did not get it. To make matters worse, the job description did not include the CPA requirement.

As my conversation with the hiring manager continued, I became angrier and frustrated with the situation. The hiring manager apologized to me for the unexpected development. He said I was the right candidate for the job, but the CEO had final say on all manager-level new hires. I was at a loss for words. I was unable to understand how an imminent offer for employment turned into such an empty pursuit. I went from the renewal phase back into the reaction phase in just one phone conversation. The negative energy overwhelmed me. I was bitterly disappointed. I knew I had to somehow overcome the situation and regain my focus on the future. I kept telling myself sometimes the best transitions are the ones you do not make.

⎯⎯◉⎯⎯

Once you learn to manage the emotional and psychological adversity of a layoff, you can gain a clearer focus. You can redirect your energy to more productive activities. This will allow you to begin moving forward toward the pursuit of new opportunities. Remember, you can control your thoughts, beliefs, and actions as well as verbal and non-verbal communication.

As you work through adversity, you should celebrate your successful progress on the emotional and psychological migration. You should do something to acknowledge your positive efforts. However, be sensible and creative in your desire to celebrate. It may not be wise to go overboard in your celebration. Rather, call a friend and go see a movie or grab a tasty dessert at your favorite ice cream shop. Remember, you need to keep moving forward after a layoff. And, mini celebrations offer effective ways of staying focused and motivated.

Even as you celebrate progress, the job search may not go as you hope or plan. Remember there are many factors impacting the job search. Competition with many other qualified candidates and economic conditions impact the recruiting and hiring processes. As a result, you may find the pursuit of a new job opportunity frustrating, if not more, than the layoff itself.

Remember, too, the emotional and psychological migration process after a layoff is often challenging and time consuming. The layoff, in some ways, is like the loss of a loved one or a friend. You need time to think and heal your emotional and psychological wounds.

No single approach or secret will help you successfully navigate the often stormy emotional and psychological migration. In personal relationships, the phrase "time heals all wounds" offers hope when you are dealing with emotional loss and trauma. In the business world, the phrase "time heals all wounds" offers a similar hope – the pursuit of the next step in the work life journey.

The way you move along the emotional and psychological migration, whether progressive or regressive, is entirely under your control. Only you can decide how and when to migrate from one phase to the next. The key is to fully understand the migration is a time-consuming process and not an overnight event. Time, patience, hope, commitment, faith, and trust – in yourself and others – are essential to making a successful emotional and psychological migration in the aftermath of a layoff.

> **Personal Challenge:**
>
> Where are you on the emotional and psychological migration?
>
> What are you doing to overcome negative energy?

Personal and Professional Relationships

Relationships are essential before, during and after a layoff – not just after the layoff. This is the premise behind the **second practical concept in the path of a lifelong work life journey – always maintain good relations with everyone – family, friends, colleagues, coworkers, business associates and acquaintances – without expecting anything in return!** The logic here is simple and straightforward – good habits and respect help build relationships and those relationships can help reveal new opportunities in the work life journey. I cannot emphasize enough the criticality behind establishing good relationships.

In business, good practice helps to build relationships, and those relationships can help build business. Many times, good relationships are the foundation of establishing successful careers. If what I am talking about sounds obvious, it is! But you would be amazed at how many people simply take relationships for granted. These people fail to understand the powerful concept of what I call *relationship reciprocity*. This refers to your willingness to respect and acknowledge others as you would have them respect and acknowledge you.

For many, relationships are merely pawns in the game of career advancement. Yet, there is so much more to learn and gain from meaningful relationships. They can provide extraordinary joy. They also can reveal opportunities to achieve long-term work life fulfillment, as opposed to the often-short-lived addiction of recognition, status, or title.

The gift of meaningful relationships is not always easily recognizable. Just as romantic relationships can take time to evolve, business relationships also need to be nurtured. Over time, a network of personal and business contacts can provide valuable opportunities to learn new things, share ideas and pursue new endeavors. In fact, a wise professor in graduate school once told me to "treat everyone you talk to as the most important person in your life at that moment."

At first, I did not understand such extraordinary advice. However, I have now learned my focus on people in my life is just as important as focusing on my goals and objectives. In other words, a simple introduction can lead to a conversation, which may turn into a more meaningful and lasting relationship over time. Therefore, make time to reach out to your network of relationships and never take such relationships for granted.

In life, you should focus more on your core principles, values, and needs, as opposed to what you want or must have due to unnecessary expectations or common greed. In relationships, it is always better to give than to receive. In personal finance, you should never spend more than you earn, but always enjoy what you spend. In business, the concepts of respect and reciprocity are fundamental requirements for achieving goals and objectives. See, the obvious is powerful indeed!

Remember, relationships often take time to develop. However, the introduction is a crucial step toward establishing a potentially long-lasting and mutually beneficial relationship. You never know when a chance meeting – at the grocery store, on an airplane or train, or in a coffee shop – can turn into an actual relationship. The fact is relationships are critical for everyone, not just those who have jobs in sales and business development.

Remember, you are also in sales. That's right, whether you believe it or not, you are actively involved in sales on a daily basis. Everything you say and do represents your knowledge and abilities. So, if you are currently employed, you must demonstrate your talents daily. If you are self-employed, you must market your skills and abilities every day. If you are in transition because of a layoff, then your duty is to market the ultimate personal brand – you!

Personal Challenge:

How do you value relationships?

How often do you "connect" with your relationships?

What do your relationships say about you?

Immediate Thoughts and Questions

For Bob, losing his job feels like starting over in some respects. He never had to look for a job during his 18-year tenure with the company. As a result, Bob faces some serious questions regarding the future:

"What will I do now?"

"How will I provide for my family?"

"How am I going to find another good job in this weak economy?"

"What am I going to tell my wife?"

"What will I say to my kids?"

Before Bob leaves the office, he dials his home number for the last time from his desk. As the phone rings, Bob continues to struggle to find the words to say to Mary, his wife of 18 years. Suddenly, Bob hears Mary's sweet voice over the phone saying, "Hi Bob. How is your morning today?" Bob remains silent for a few seconds to collect his thoughts and finally says, "Sweetheart, do you have any lunch plans today?" "No," she replies, "I was just planning to stay home today."

Bob gathers every ounce of strength to hold back the tears and avoid any cracking sound in his voice. "Well, how about if I come home for lunch today?" Mary is happy Bob will be coming home for lunch and quickly begins preparing a special meal for them to enjoy.

Sally, on the other hand, is alone during her layoff crisis. Her daughter, Ashley, is in class at the local high school. Although Sally has endured hardship for most of her life, she has always provided as well as possible for her daughter. Today, however, Sally is suddenly faced with a problem that has no immediate solution.

She is concerned about how Ashley will react to the bad news. Will Ashley be afraid of the future? Sally does not want to give her daughter any reason for concern. However, they have a close relationship; they talk about everything – school, boys, love, family, and the future.

Ashley wants to attend college and then medical school to pursue her dream of becoming a pediatrician. Sally begins to ask herself some tough questions:

"Why has this happened to me?"

"What will I do next?"

"How will I provide for my daughter?"

"How will I continue to make her dreams come true?"

"Where will I find another job like the one I just lost?"

"Who will hire me without a degree?"

Soon after leaving the plant for the last time, Vince finds himself in good company with a bottle of hard liquor at the local pub. There are several other patrons at the pub drinking, eating, and playing pool. Vince is noticeably angry and feeling quite depressed with his layoff, which has turned his life upside down. Many questions and thoughts begin to haunt Vince regarding his immediate future:

"What will I tell my wife?"

"How will I provide for my family?"

"What will I do next?"

"Where will I find another job?"

"How will I pay my bills?"

⎯⎯◉⎯⎯

The questions Bob, Sally, and Vince ask themselves are on the minds of many people confronting a disruption in their work life journey – the layoff. These are people with genuine concerns and real problems. Have you have encountered such a mentally exhausting situation? I hope not. As for me, I have dealt with the layoff situation on more than one occasion. Although you cannot change the past, you can address the present, and hopefully influence the future.

⎯⎯◉⎯⎯

Move Forward from the Layoff

Monday, January 5th, 11 AM – Before Bob goes home, he takes a walk outside. Although the temperature is a chilly 25 degrees, it is an otherwise clear and pleasant day. There is a walking trail, which wraps around the entire office complex nestled in a wooded area. Many people traverse this trail to get some fresh air and exercise.

After his walk around the office, Bob gets in his car, puts on his sunglasses and heads home. As Mary sits in a comfy upholstered chair next to beautiful custom curtains adorning the large living room window, her eyes well up with tears because of an earlier phone conversation with a dear friend. The kids are in school, and the mail carrier is pulling away after delivering the mail.

As Mary sees Bob pull into the driveway, she makes her way through the kitchen and laundry rooms to the garage door entrance. The second Mary sees Bob she starts to smile. Bob sees how happy Mary is to see him, walks over to her and gives her a kiss and a firm hug. On any other day, their greeting would be perfectly normal, but today their loving embrace takes on a whole new meaning for Bob.

"Hi sweetheart, it's so good to see you," Bob whispers in Mary's ear. "Bob, are you OK?" Mary asks. "I'm afraid I have some bad news. I had a meeting with my boss this morning. My job was eliminated today," Bob explains. Before Bob can say anything further, Mary asks, "Are you serious? What happened? My friend Janice's husband also lost his job last week. Did you know this was going to happen? Oh, listen to me going on and on; honey, it's OK; we will get through this together." At this moment, Bob experiences the entire spectrum of emotions – from disappointment and emptiness on one end to understanding, compassion, and love on the other.

Bob believes with Mary's help he will overcome the latest challenge in his life. With an accounting degree, and an active certified public accountant (CPA) license, Bob has the technical knowledge to continue his career with another organization. However, day by day, more and more companies are announcing layoffs, and Bob knows he is not alone in the quest to overcome a layoff.

Monday, January 5th, 12 PM – Sally collects her personal items from her office cubicle and begins the slow walk to her car. On the way, she pauses near the desks of some colleagues to say a few parting words. As Sally approaches the main entrance of the building, she stops and turns around to take one final look at the place she has called home away from home for the past 18 years. Still in a state of disbelief, Sally exits the building one last time.

Usually, Sally goes straight home from the office. But today, she decides to go to the local coffee shop before heading home. Sally is a frequent visitor to the trendy coffee shop, and the owner and other employees know her very well. However, this is the first-time Sally has visited the coffee shop during lunchtime on a weekday. Joe, the coffee shop owner, is happy to see Sally, who quietly proceeds to the back-corner chair and table, her favorite spot.

In an instant, Joe knows something is not quite right with Sally. She doesn't seem to have the same jovial spirit. Without asking, Joe gives Sally the usual – a large white chocolate mocha latte with skim milk. Before Sally can reach for her wallet, Joe smiles and says, "Sally, it's on the house." "Thank you so much Joe," Sally says in a subdued voice.

The coffee shop is quiet today, as only a few other customers are inside. Joe continues to wonder why Sally seems so concerned. Finally, he asks, "Is everything OK?" Sally looks at Joe, and after a few seconds says, "Things could be better, Joe. I just lost the job I had for 18 years. I have no idea what happened. I am still just trying to make sense of it," she says.

Sally is hopeful she can overcome the layoff situation, but she needs to address some personal matters in the immediate future. First of all, she knows she must somehow complete her college studies and finally earn the elusive degree. She understands earning a degree would provide a much better chance to compete with other job candidates in the marketplace.

However, Sally is also worried about her daughter's future education. How can Sally afford to complete her studies, while simultaneously preparing for her daughter's educational dreams? Sally is once again overwhelmed and emotional; there are so many more questions and concerns than answers, and the road to recovery seems so daunting and far away.

Monday, January 5th, 5 PM - Vince avoids going home and having to share his disappointing news with his family. Instead, Vince calls his best friend Jake and asks him to meet at the local pub.

Soon after Jake arrives at the pub; Vince begins to share his angry thoughts and emotions about the layoff. "I can't believe what's happened; I gave the company 17 years of hard work. I never complained; I just did my job, day in and day out, and this how those heartless bastards treat me," Vince shouts out in anger.

"I am so sorry man; there just isn't any loyalty these days" Jake says in return.

As he patiently listens to Vince express his emotions, Jake struggles to find a way to help his best friend. "Hey, we've been through a whole lot together over the years, and I am here for you buddy," Jake says in a somber voice. "What can I do? Just name it," Jake says. Vince appreciates the gesture but realizes he must overcome his anger and deal with the situation. This means Vince must first, somehow, gather the strength and courage to go home and discuss the situation with his wife, Susan.

When Vince arrives home, Susan is busy cooking, and his son is watching cartoons in the family room. Almost immediately, Susan knows something is wrong, as Vince is not his usual goofy self. "Hi Babe," Vince struggles to find any other words to greet Susan. He grabs a beer from the fridge and looks at his high school sweetheart. After a large gulp of beer, he begins to tell Susan he was laid off from work.

At first, Susan does not take Vince seriously. "You're joking, right?" Vince looks down and says nothing in return. As Susan tries to make sense of the situation, she almost burns her hands on the cooking pot. "That's just great, what the hell are we going to do now?" she says.

Susan understands Vince is upset and sad. However, she is overwhelmed with fear and anxiety. Suddenly, a few words turn into a stormy argument. They start yelling at each other using harsh words. Vince grabs another beer from the fridge and sits down at the kitchen table. Susan just looks out the window and begins to cry. Although the layoff is not Vince's fault, Susan is caught up in her own emotions.

Meanwhile, Dillon walks into the kitchen in tears because he overhears the argument between his parents. "Mommy, Daddy, please don't' yell at each other," Dillon says sadly. Vince and Susan realize they must gain control of their emotions. They must focus on taking the necessary steps to get back on track without causing Dillon any more grief. "Look at us. I can't believe we argued in front of Dillon," Susan whispers to Vince. "I'm sorry, Babe, I didn't mean for any of this to happen. You and Dillon mean the world to me," Vince says. "I promise we will get through this somehow, some way," Vince reassures Susan.

Like many people, Vince is a proud man. He is too embarrassed to seek help from others during this obvious time of need. However, Vince does have several good friends in town, a few who are like brothers.

He needs to focus on a positive future with his wife and son no matter what happens. Vince's friends will also play a huge role in keeping his spirits high, while trying to find the next job in his work life journey. But first, Vince needs to release his negative energy before he seeks any help from his friends.

Bob, Sally, and Vince are people with diverse backgrounds who each must confront the harsh reality of a layoff. The layoff is not something they are ready to accept. However, they all start the emotional and psychological migration by realizing and facing the myriad of emotions and thoughts upon receiving notice of their layoff.

In fact, Bob, Sally, and Vince do not realize it at the time, but their simple conversations with family and friends launch the recovery process, and migration from the reaction phase to the reflection phase. This allows them to begin reflecting on their personal situations in their own ways. Bob, Sally, and Vince recall rough patches in their lives, but never something quite like a layoff.

Reflection

"The journey of a thousand miles must begin with a single step."
Chinese Proverb

What Is Your Brand?

When was the last time you thought of yourself as a "brand?" Think about the products and services you purchase or use on a daily, weekly, or monthly basis. For example, you may prefer a particular brand of coffee for your daily caffeine break. Or, perhaps you prefer a specific brand for mobile phone and tablet devices. Or, perhaps a specific brand is your favorite athletic sports brand. So, ask yourself, why do you like specific brands over other comparable brands? What are the qualities or attributes of the brands that influence your buying decisions? I purchase brands based on quality, reliability, innovation, and of course the perceived value the brands have to offer.

Just as the branding concept is vital to organizations that offer products and services for customers worldwide, your "personal brand" represents what you have to offer to others in your work life journey. In other words, your personal brand influences and determines how others think, believe, and feel about your appearance, character, image, personality, skills, knowledge, and experience.

As you navigate the work life journey, you may encounter opportunities, challenges, or unexpected detours that can have a profound impact on your personal brand. Therefore, it is crucial to establish, nurture, and manage your personal brand, because your personal brand is always on display. One way to better understand and appreciate the criticality of your personal brand is to embrace and apply what I call the B.R.A.N.D. concept, where:

B – Believe (confidence in yourself so that others believe in you too)

R – Reputation (skills, subject matter expertise that establish your credibility)

A – Adaptability (willingness to adapt to changing priorities and opportunities)

N – Networking (focus on establishing and maintaining relationships)

D – Determination (commitment to pursuing a successful professional journey)

One simple, quick, and effective way to better identify and understand your personal brand is to complete the following exercise:

Determine one-word brand attributes that best describe your personal brand. For example, the attributes that best define and describe my personal brand include communication, dependable, resourceful, and collaborative. Try this exercise; I have shared this exercise with several friends and colleagues, and they all found the exercise thought-provoking, helpful, and revealing.

Another effective way to enhance and manage your personal brand is to periodically perform a "self-audit" using the following basic questions:

Do others say positive things about you?

How do others describe your talents and abilities?

Do others come to you for guidance/advice?

What new knowledge/experience have you gained?

Do others recommend or endorse you?

Do others consider you a credible person or valued team member?

Remember, your education, experience, subject matter expertise, skills suggest that you are well-qualified, *but it is your personal brand that will set you apart* from others. I recommend you perform a self-audit of your brand at least once a year; I review my personal brand a minimum of two times per year.

Timeout

After a layoff, the first thing to do is do nothing! Let me say it again, *the first thing to do is nothing*. OK. Calm down. I am not crazy. The last thing you want is to do something in a highly emotional state of mind. You think, behave, and act more rationally if you just take some time to reflect on what has happened. Now, don't get me wrong, I am not suggesting you sit and dwell on the past forever. Rather, you need to take a reasonable timeout to gain proper perspective. This is the essence behind the **third practical concept to remember in your work life journey – maintain a positive mental attitude always, but particularly after a layoff.**

The primary purpose for a timeout is to focus on something other than the layoff. Some people keep a daily journal, which by the way is a good idea. The daily journal is a way to express your thoughts and feelings about the layoff. However, you may not have the time, nor make time, to write about meaningful moments on a daily basis. Therefore, a practical alternative is to pursue some personal down time, when you stop thinking about the layoff and focus on other positive things like family, friends, or fun hobbies and activities.

Just how much time you need to get away and relax is up to you. Having said that, pay attention to the concept of time. In other words, when a layoff happens, it is reasonable to spend a few days to clear your mind. However, avoid the trap of dwelling on the layoff for weeks or months. Remember, it is important to clear your mind, so you focus your energy on moving forward with constructive activities, goals, and objectives. A clear mind is an ideal starting point for establishing a fresh, positive attitude after a layoff.

After my first layoff, I had a short conversation with Brad, an acquaintance I met at a networking event. Brad talked to me about his "vacation" after he was laid off. Just a week after his layoff he went camping in Wisconsin with a couple of friends. The weather was still warm enough to enjoy the outdoors, and the forest was beginning to blossom in a flurry of traditional autumn colors. Brad was single and for the most part free of major financial obligations. He lived in an apartment and used public transportation for his daily commuting needs.

Now, you may think a road trip after a layoff was not necessary for Brad. If you do, then you have missed the point. I am not saying you have to get away to clear your mind. You may not have the opportunity to get away like Brad did. However, the concept of getting away can offer an ideal opportunity to overcome the negative energy created by the layoff. For Brad, the camping adventure was a mental and emotional retreat. It was designed to free his mind from the negativity of the layoff and re-energize him to take the next steps in his work life journey.

———◉———

Physical exercise is another excellent way to release negative energy. Regular physical activity enables the body to produce *endorphins*, which are powerful all-natural chemical reactions. The endorphins create positive energy in your body and improve overall wellness. Physical exercise can also result in better health and mental state. Some people go to the gym. Others jog or take up yoga, biking, or power walking. The point is to find your method of reflection so you can clear your mind and focus on the challenge ahead – the job search.

Another positive way to reflect and gain proper perspective is by participating in local volunteer efforts. There are several potential venues for volunteering in your local community: religious establishments such as churches, synagogues, or temples; community clubs and programs; and school events. **Volunteer opportunities can help take your mind off the layoff, while allowing you to make a positive contribution to help other people or worthy causes – the fourth practical concept to keep in mind in the work life journey.**

For me, my personal sanctuary was working with my wife to prepare for the upcoming birth of our first child – just after my first layoff. That was probably the low point in my professional journey, until several years later, when I was laid off for the second time. On each occasion, I was overwhelmed by the same questions facing Bob, Sally, Vince and all who have endured the emptiness of a layoff.

Yet, in the aftermath of my first layoff, I found it difficult to think about my loss, when the entire country was dealing with tragic events of the September 11, 2001 terrorist attacks. In fact, my sister and I were on airplanes when the attacks occurred. I cannot imagine how my wife and mother felt as the tragedy unfolded that unforgettable day. While my sister and I both landed safely at our respective destinations, I was caught off guard by a single voicemail. The voicemail was from my wife. She was in tears asking me to call her because planes were "falling out of the sky!"

Soon after the 9/11 attacks, my employer announced the largest layoff in the history of the company. Overnight, more than half the company staff was laid off. There were no words to describe the collective emotion expressed by all those impacted by such a massive corporate workforce reduction. There was plenty of sadness and anger among those laid off.

At the time, I was sad, disappointed, and angry. Yet, there was little time for me to waste feeling miserable, for the birth of my first child was literally just a few precious months away. When my son finally arrived, nothing mattered more to me than he did. I still recall the day in the hospital when I held my newborn son in my hands for the very first time. I was overwhelmed with pure joy.

Somehow, the loss of my job was no longer a focal point of my life. Rather, it was this little bundle of joy wrapped snuggly in a warm blanket and sleeping peacefully in my arms. Of course, the reality of not being employed crept back into my mind soon thereafter. But, I had a clear mind regarding the immediate tasks ahead. First, I had to answer many of the same questions Bob, Sally and Vince were confronting in their situations. Next, I had to update my inventory of personal attributes, as well as my resume, which I will discuss later.

I took a personal oath to do whatever was necessary to create a bright future for my family. The challenge became overcoming the staggering impact of an economic environment shaken to its very core. Many companies continued to lay off people and suspend recruiting and hiring activities. I had no idea when the economy would improve or when hiring would resume.

As I continued the job search, I pursued avenues not necessarily related to any job I held before. For example, I taught communication and various introductory computer classes at a local junior college. I also helped others with resume and interview preparation. In addition, I took time to think about how my knowledge, skills and experience could be applied in other industries or vocations. While I continued my efforts in the consulting industry, I also considered acquiring additional knowledge and skills. Remember, the one powerful way you can develop your personal brand is by differentiating yourself from the competition – others also looking to make meaningful transitions in the work life journey.

I also developed and facilitated project management training seminars for clients in Chicago, Los Angeles, San Francisco, Seattle, and New Jersey. The frequent travel and "live performances" were time consuming and energy depleting. However, the focus was to leverage my experience into a more stable and reliable source of income. More importantly, the periodic training and teaching schedule gave me a reason to look forward to the future. The training and teaching introduced me to many people from different industries and walks of life. As I think back on those days, such chance meetings were valuable indeed.

———⬤———

For Bob, the first action after his layoff was appropriate; he called his wife. Although he did not know it at the time, Bob started the process to address and overcome the layoff situation with that call. The first thing Sally did after the layoff was visit the coffee shop and talk to Joe, which was a positive step in her emotional and psychological migration. Vince also took a positive step by calling his best friend to begin diffusing an otherwise emotionally charged situation.

Personal Challenge:

How did you take "timeout" after your layoff?

How did you feel after your "timeout?"

What actions did you take after your "timeout"?

CDA Principle

A layoff is a life changing event. The spectrum of emotions, coupled with psychological anxiety, can create an aura of negativity and despair. This negative energy must not overtake your ability to think ahead and move forward. There is a saying, "people do not plan to fail; they fail to plan." We cannot move forward without thinking forward first.

Believe it or not, a layoff presents a new beginning – a chance for a fresh start – at a new organization or industry or both. However, making a successful new career transition requires a clear understanding of what I call "**The CDA Principle**" – **the fifth practical concept to embrace in the work life journey.** CDA stands for confidence, discipline, and attitude – the foundational building blocks for making successful work life transitions enroute to achieving personal and professional fulfillment.

Confidence is the first, and most critical, component of the CDA principle. Before anyone can believe in you and your skills and abilities, *you must first believe in yourself.* This concept sounds easy but is often quite challenging – even for the most experienced and skilled professionals. Confidence is like knowledge – it takes time to develop and grow. With time, confidence can grow strong and offer the opportunity to pursue new challenges and achieve new accomplishments.

However, confidence is a difficult concept to comprehend, much less harness. For me, confidence is like an internal on/off switch. You have this internal switch that you need to turn on. While everyone has the confidence switch, the point is to find the switch first – and then flip it on, and then keep it on.

There are several ways to help raise your level of confidence and keep you focused during the job search:

- Stick to a daily routine and schedule.
- Get out and about; avoid staying home glued to the computer or television.
- Talk to your close friends frequently.
- Seek the wisdom and guidance of a mentor.
- Think about your role models.
- Stay abreast of developments in your industry or area of expertise.
- Focus on your strengths (i.e., skills, knowledge, expertise etc.)
- Listen to, or attend, motivational training programs or seminars.
- Consider volunteer opportunities.
- Explore other projects, activities, or hobbies.
- Join professional networking groups.
- Pursue new learning opportunities to enhance your knowledge and repertoire of skills.

Discipline is the second key component of the CDA principle. Think about all the things you do on a daily basis, things you rarely consider. For example, you brush your teeth, take a shower, get ready and make time to eat. A daily routine is a form of daily discipline.

However, I want to focus on the plan, effort and activities designed to achieve specific goals and objectives, like making a successful work life transition after a layoff. In this context, discipline represents the plan, structure or schedule, dedication, and determination to follow-through on the tasks at hand. In the job search process, discipline is a true catalyst in finding and pursuing the next work life transition.

For example, you need to stay positive, expand your network of contacts, and continue developing your skills and enhancing your knowledge. These examples represent the fundamental premise behind discipline. In the end, discipline is about your commitment to make something positive happen – like executing the job search process.

Attitude is the third and final component of the CDA principle. Attitude plays a key role in everything we do and achieve or not. In other words, attitude is a catalyst to greater self-confidence. Many books and research studies focus on the powerful concept known as attitude and its impact on confidence and achievement of goals and objectives.

While those books and studies offer a great deal of information, it is you who must recognize the ability to harness the power of attitude. Your attitude should guide you toward the achievement of personal and professional goals. Did you know it takes the same amount of energy to think positively as it does to think negatively? Yet, many suffer the paralysis of negative thinking during times when positive thinking is needed most – after a layoff.

Once a layoff occurs, your network of contacts – family, friends, and business colleagues – can offer help. You should reach out to your close contacts. However, it is critical to visually and verbally demonstrate your confidence and positive attitude to ensure people in your network understand you believe in your abilities.

Personal Challenge:

How would you rate yourself according to the CDA Principle?

Where can you improve?

What actions are you taking to improve?

Seek Guidance from a Mentor

I have learned over the course of my career the work life journey is filled with challenge, joy, disappointment and sometimes emptiness. Yet, you must find a way to overcome adversity while maintaining a strong belief in your ability to move forward and achieve personal and professional goals and objectives. You may have many questions about your work life journey, but you may not always have the answers.

As you navigate through this journey called life, there are times when anxiety, fear and even uncertainty may keep you from moving forward. There are times when you may focus on destinations as opposed to the specific steps or actions necessary to achieve your goals. It is during these times when a *mentor* is someone who can offer much needed guidance and direction.

———◦◦———

Over the course of my career, I have been fortunate to meet some wonderful and talented people who took time out of their busy schedules to take an interest in my career pursuits. I still recall the conversation I had many years ago with a colleague named Russ. At the time, I was a senior consultant with one of the largest accounting, auditing, and management consulting firms in the world. While performing business risk management work, I discovered a new passion – the desire to pursue a career in training and speaking to audiences of diverse sizes. I found myself at a crossroad in my career. I was excited and confused at the same time.

To this day, I am grateful to Russ for his willingness to listen to my evolving career interests. Russ also gave me the guidance to consider how I could pursue my newfound passion without adversely impacting my existing role within the firm. From that initial conversation, Russ became a career mentor and friend I trust and respect to this very day.

Mentors, like coaches, can have a profound impact on your work life journey because they are able to objectively evaluate your strengths and weaknesses, as well as your interests. True mentors avoid making hasty judgments. Rather, mentors are in a unique position to offer constructive criticism regarding the evolution of your work life journey. **I encourage you to find a trustworthy mentor in your life – the sixth practical concept to remember in your work life journey.**

True mentors can assess your personality and abilities. Based on this information, mentors can make practical suggestions to help you prepare for the next step in your work life journey. Although your focus after a layoff is on finding the next permanent job, a mentor may suggest you pursue other opportunities as well. For example, temporary or contract-based jobs offer very good avenues to demonstrate your abilities. You also can gain valuable experience across multiple employers. These roles may lead to permanent jobs.

So, ask yourself – who is your mentor? When was the last time you had a meaningful conversation with your mentor? Just as an athlete seeks guidance from his or her coach, you should consider establishing mentor relationships to periodically assess your evolving work life journey. Mentors can help you put your past, your current role, and your future plans or goals into focus. For this reason, a mentor should be someone you respect and trust. And, a mentor should also be someone you stay in touch with periodically – not just in times of need like after a layoff.

Personal Challenge:

Who is your mentor?

How often do you "connect" with your mentor?

Are you a mentor to someone? If not, why not?

Think about Your Role Models

While mentors can provide guidance, role models can offer inspiration. **It is helpful to think about roles models that have had a profound impact on your life or inspired you in some way – the seventh practical concept to remember in the work life journey.** A role model is someone you believe has achieved the kind of success you aspire to. By the way, a role model does not have to be someone in a leadership or authoritative position. In fact, a role model can be anyone with the following characteristics:

- A strong work ethic.
- A passion for the job he/she does.
- A genuine desire to help others.
- A focus on personal and professional development.
- A commitment to achieve goals and objectives.

Think about all the people you know, or have met, in your life. Chances are you have come across someone who has inspired you or influenced your thoughts and beliefs. Who is that person? Is it a member of your family? Is it your current or former boss? Is it a friend or business colleague? Or, maybe your role model is a favorite teacher you had in high school or college. I bet your role model is also someone you respect and admire.

For me, a wonderful man named Jay has been my role model throughout my work life journey. Jay was born and raised on a rural farm in Asia during the time of World War II. He was one of five children and learned the concepts of discipline and hard work at a very early age. In addition to plenty of homework from school, there were many chores to do on the farm. In fact, Jay often tells me about how little time he and his siblings had for just having fun.

Jay's parents earned a modest living, which is to say finances were just enough to meet basic needs and not much more. However, the home was a warm environment filled with love and joy. Above all, home was a place based on good values and beliefs among all family members – love, understanding, honesty, and helping others. Jay's parents always asked their children to give their best effort in everything, from schoolwork to farm work, and to always be respectful of others.

Back in those childhood and teenage years, Jay did not have the benefit of powerful and convenient farm machinery and equipment for farming chores. He also did not have a personal computer or the Internet to help with schoolwork. He and his brothers and sisters completed their tasks the old-fashioned way – hard, time-consuming manual labor and effort. While Jay performed his daily activities and responsibilities without complaints, he believed life had more to offer. However, Jay had many questions and very few answers. Each day, he focused on school and excelled in his classes from elementary school through college and post-graduate studies.

As a young man in his early twenties, Jay was at a crossroads in his life. He needed to determine the direction and path for his future. Jay sought advice and guidance from elders in his community. After much discussion and deliberation, and at the recommendation of the elders, Jay decided to further his education in mathematics and computer science. He was strongly encouraged to continue his quest for knowledge and experience in the United States. To this day, Jay considers himself quite fortunate for the guidance and strong encouragement he received from his family and elders in his hometown.

Eventually, Jay arrived in Dallas, Texas, where he attended graduate school. He worked odd jobs to pay the bills, while always focusing on the next chapter in his work life journey. Life back in those days had many challenges, and Jay had his share of corporate hurdles, too. To complicate matters further, Jay and his wife had a one-year-old son. I still recall the story about Jay not being able to afford a simple ice cream cone for his son. Back then, the price of an ice cream cone was only 10 cents. However, Jay and his wife kept the faith, believed in each other, and were determined to create a better life for their son.

The next chapter in Jay's life became a reality in Chicago, where he landed his first full-time job with a large manufacturing and information technology company. From those early formative years in his career, Jay worked diligently to establish himself as a loyal and dedicated employee. He focused on helping the IT department, and the company, achieve goals and objectives. Jay worked his way up to a management level in the company before he decided to pursue a more challenging opportunity at a small specialty manufacturing company.

Once again, Jay proved his worth on a daily basis. His work ethic and talent earned him a promotion to director of management information systems. The values Jay learned back on the farm as a child paid real dividends later in life. He was living the American dream.

Jay's entire career is best characterized by one powerful concept – "always give your 110% at everything you do and never let expectations dictate your beliefs or govern your actions." In other words, focus on the journey, not the destination. Focus on the effort, not the reward. Focus on personal fulfillment, not professional title. Jay is one of the most dedicated and diligent people I have ever known. In fact, I still think he gets more done during the early morning hours of a day than most other people do in an entire day. For this reason, I think Jay would have made a great commander in the military.

Jay's beliefs and values continue to have a profound impact on my life. With any luck, I can only hope I instill such values and beliefs with my three children. To this day, I consider myself truly fortunate if I can be half as wise and successful as Jay. I have been through two layoffs in my professional journey. And, each time I reached out to Jay for his guidance and advice.

While I was focused on finding the next step in my professional journey, Jay on the other hand took time to guide me through his personal stories. Those stories inspired me to reflect and gain a better perspective on life in general. In other words, Jay has always been my life advisor. I am forever indebted to him for his wisdom, guidance, patience, and most of all love – for *Jay is someone very dear to me. He is my dad and the person I most admire.*

My dad has many stories about what it takes to manage your personal and work life journey. There is one recurring theme in all his stories – the meaning and value behind relationships with family, friends, colleagues, and most importantly God. My dad is a people person and believes relationships offer many lessons, which can benefit you for a lifetime. He often reminds me we can only control what we think, believe, say, and do. Everything else is outside our control. As human beings, we do not always understand there is a purpose behind every action or event happening in our world. My dad will forever be a source of inspiration and guidance. His philosophy and perspectives on life, work and just about everything else help shape my mindset for the future.

| **Personal Challenge:** |
| Who is your role model? |
| Why is he/she your role model? |

Establish a Daily Routine

As if the emotional trauma of the layoff is not already enough to deal with, you need to find ways to stay productive and just keep your sanity. Therefore, you need to take time to reflect and clear your mind. Once you have a sensible state of mind, the next step is to begin thinking about simple activities you can do on a daily basis. For example, I catch up on current news – global, national, and local – every morning. From there, I follow a daily schedule.

After my layoff, I devoted at least four hours a day to planning, executing, and monitoring my job search activities. Some of these tasks can be done at home, while others require you to venture out. The process of finding the next job after a layoff is like having a full-time job. So, **establish a consistent schedule or routine with daily and weekly activities and responsibilities to help make the job search process more effective – the eighth practical concept to remember in the work life journey.**

Many people stay home or avoid going out as much as possible during a layoff. This will not help you. You should not just stay home after a layoff. You need to get out and about. You need to be seen and heard. You need to stay connected with the local business marketplace. The silent, stay at home approach does not often yield measurable results.

The job search process can be as intense and time-consuming as you make it. You decide how many phone calls to make and e-mails to write. You decide how to pursue networking activities – reaching out and meeting with people you know or want to meet. When I was laid off, I connected with my network of contacts often – over the phone and in person as often as possible. You need to demonstrate your active desire to move forward from a layoff. Remember to send a thank you e-mail or note to people for their willingness to meet with you.

As you pursue and complete daily job search tasks and activities, you should keep track of your efforts and progress. You can use a daily planner book or spreadsheet to document and monitor your activities. Your daily planner or spreadsheet can also serve as an effective motivational tool as you move forward in the emotional and psychological migration.

For Bob and Mary, the daily goal is to continue building their network of contacts. Bob has a goal of scheduling at least two informational interviews or network touch points every day. These meetings can be formal or informal. Bob and Mary also play active roles in community social events – school gatherings and activities, church events, as well as the weekly bowling league night with their close friends. Bob's layoff is a disruption in his professional journey. However, the other aspects of life stay the same and should remain unchanged as part of a routine schedule.

As for Sally, she plays an active role in her church, which has been a genuine source of strength throughout her life, but particularly after her recent layoff. Sally also volunteers at the local YMCA because she loves working with young children to help build their confidence. She wants to instill good values in the children and be a positive role model for them.

Sally enjoys spending time with her friends. They play cards, watch movies, and take turns hosting "cooking night." Each week a different person prepares, discusses, and shares a new recipe. During the layoff, Sally expands her network by visiting the coffee shop every day. She quickly learns she is not alone in the layoff crisis.

Not long after Vince is laid off, he begins to offer his time and skills to others in the community. Although Vince is most experienced in blue-collar labor, he is also very smart in math. In fact, one of Vince's friends has a cousin who is the assistant principal at the local elementary school. With the help of his friend's cousin, Vince schedules a meeting with the assistant principal to discuss how he could provide part-time, voluntary math tutoring services to the students. Vince finds joy and strength in helping others in his community. He is also a good handyperson, which he believes will provide additional opportunities to find temporary, meaningful work.

As Vince provides tutoring services and performs a few handyperson projects, he also keeps his eyes and ears open for the next job in his work life journey. However, Vince's biggest challenge is just staying positive because he has no leads for a permanent job. Day after day, the economic news is getting worse, and Vince needs to find ways to stay focused on his job search.

Assess the Financial Situation

At some point after the layoff, the reality of not receiving a paycheck hits home hard. For Bob, Sally and Vince, life without a paycheck is now a painful reality. It amazes me just how fragile the financial picture is without a steady stream of income. Today, we live in a society struggling with the concept of saving money. If we are to create a good future for our children and generations thereafter, then we must focus on establishing good habits and financial discipline today. This means you need to live within your budget.

Friday, January 9th – Bob and Mary sit at the kitchen table to put the financial picture in better focus. They begin by itemizing their current financial situation. Mary creates a spreadsheet to list all current financial obligations. Table 2 illustrates the financial obligations Bob and Mary currently have.

Table 2 – Itemized Financial Obligations

Financial Obligation	Monthly Payment
Mortgage	$1,535
Car Loan	$455
Credit Cards	$200
Utilities	$375

Keep in mind, Table 2 only presents the fixed monthly costs. Bob and Mary also have several variable costs, which include fuel for the cars, groceries, as well as other miscellaneous expenses. Once all financial obligations have been identified, the next step is to account for all available sources of cash:

- Bank accounts (i.e., checking, savings, money market etc.).
- Investment accounts (i.e., stocks, bonds, and/or other financial instruments).
- Personal assets (i.e., jewelry, diamonds, and/or other valuables).
- Retirement accounts (i.e., 401k, IRA, and/or other accounts).

Sally also has real monthly financial obligations. Rent, utilities, and credit cards are the largest monthly expenses for Sally. Fortunately, she is being frugal with credit card purchases. However, in this economy, even a small credit card balance can have a long-lasting impact. As a single mother and lone income-earner, Sally has not been able to save diligently over the years. Consequently, Sally's stress level rises like the mercury on a hot afternoon in the middle of summer.

There is the added pressure of providing a good educational future for her daughter. On a positive note, Sally is a courageous and positive person. Although her financial picture is now more uncertain, without a job, Sally believes she and her daughter will be OK for the next four months. Sally's faith, commitment, and perseverance will help her through this tough time.

Vince also has his share of fixed bills and other monthly expenses. Together with his wife Susan, Vince looks at the family budget. They know they must cut back on expenses wherever possible. So, Vince will not visit the local pub as often as he did before the layoff. And most importantly, Vince and Susan understand they need to make the necessary sacrifices to ensure their son can continue his daily routine without interruption. Dillon's future means everything to Vince and Susan.

As Vince and Susan review the budget, they realize just how critical their situation is with the mortgage, car payment, utilities, and a new high-definition television. Susan asks, "Vince, what if you cannot find a job soon? What are we going to do?" she asks, beginning to cry again. Vince gives her a comforting hug. Although they are OK for now, he, too, is overwhelmed with fear and sadness.

As Susan begins to share the awful stories of people in her office who lost everything because of losing their jobs, Vince quickly interrupts her. He reassures Susan, telling her he will do everything in his power to make sure they all get through this difficult situation. "It will not be easy, but the important thing is we have each other," Vince says in a calm and considerate tone. "And, as long as we have each other, we will be fine, I promise," Vince says, embracing Susan again.

———— ◉ ————

I still remember the conversation I had with my wife after my first layoff. We were expecting the birth of our first child, and I lost my job. Fortunately for us, my wife still had a job. After maternity leave, we asked our parents to help with our son. My wife continued to work, and I focused on my professional development training practice. I also was looking for another permanent full-time job. Life was never the same again. Life was a struggle back then, but we learned to enjoy each other and live within our budget.

To this day, we have not forgotten the daily challenge from the first layoff. And, it is a good thing because we suffered our second layoff while I was writing this book. But now, the stakes are much higher than they were during the first layoff. We are now a family of five, as our older son has twin siblings. Nevertheless, our faith, commitment and attitude continue to guide us through another challenging time in our lives.

When a layoff occurs, many concerns surface and become harsh realities. The current financial situation and future financial outlook are usually at the top of the "causes for concern" list. Remember, there is never a good time for a layoff. And, most people are not ready emotionally, psychologically, or financially when a layoff occurs. The daily stress of looking for a new job is now eclipsed by the emotional and psychological trauma of losing a regular paycheck. It is only natural to be concerned about the present and to feel stress about the future:

"How will the bills be paid?"

"What will happen if you cannot find another job soon?"

Remember, the layoff is a life-changing event. It requires a careful assessment of the current financial situation, as well as future financial priorities and decisions. As a rule of thumb, it is a wise practice to have a four- to six-month financial reserve set aside to address a life-changing event such as a layoff. While it may not always be feasible to have such a reserve, the key is to focus on establishing the reserve and funding it whenever possible. You never know when the reserve will be needed.

Personal Challenge:

What is your financial situation?

How often do you review your budget?

Do you have good financial discipline?

Inventory of Personal Attributes

Let me state a simple truth: you have knowledge, experience, and skills. Others may have more knowledge, greater experience, and additional skills. Nevertheless, you have something to offer the next employer in the work life journey. Therefore, the real challenge is finding the employer who will recognize your personal brand and what you have to offer. However, before you can share what you know, you need to identify and understand your strengths and abilities.

This leads me to the **ninth practical concept to embrace in the work life journey, which is to clearly identify and understand your inventory of personal attributes – key strengths, weaknesses, knowledge/subject matter expertise, skills, likes and dislikes.** As creatures of habit, we tend to defer such an "illuminating" activity until it becomes an absolute necessity – after the loss of a job. Truth is, you should frequently review your personal brand; once a year is the minimum, but a quarterly assessment is better. In fact, you need to document your inventory of personal attributes throughout the course of your work life journey. This concept is also referred to as a comprehensive self-assessment. Table 3 is an example illustration of an inventory of personal attributes.

Table 3 – Sample Inventory of Personal Attributes

Personal Attribute	Description	Ranking
Strengths	Team player	High
Weaknesses	Perfectionist	Low
Knowledge/subject matter expertise	Financial Close	High
Skills	Leadership, project management	High
Likes	Financial analysis	High
Dislikes	Management	Low

A complete inventory of personal attributes takes time to develop. You need to go back in time and recall the personal attributes you developed over the course of your work life journey. This is part one of your personal inventory. While it is not important to have an equal number of items for each attribute category, it is important to address each category with at least one item. And, do not forget to think about the odd jobs you held during high school and college. Those jobs may have exposed you to an array of personal attributes you otherwise would have overlooked.

For example, while I was in high school and college, my first job was as a sales associate for an upscale retail store where I learned valuable customer service skills. However, I also learned about the retail industry, marketing, and inventory management. By working and studying at the same time, I also learned critical organization and time management skills.

Part two of your personal inventory is the ranking of each personal attribute. For example, the most important skill for me is communication – the lifeline for every relationship in my life, personally and professionally. There is no need to use an elaborate system to rank each personal attribute; just use a practical common-sense approach such as high, medium, and low (as illustrated in Table 3).

No one knows your personal attributes better than you. Not all attributes need to be ranked as "high." However, if there are attributes you consider important but are ranked "low," then you may want to seek opportunities to strengthen those attributes.

I often tell people to start with what you do not like or do not want to identify what you do like or want. For example, you may not like or want to manage other people. This does not imply you do not like other people. Rather, you just do not want supervisory or managerial roles and responsibilities. This is OK. Management positions are not for everyone. By identifying the skills and/or activities you do not like or want, you can then focus your time and effort on isolating the skills and activities you most enjoy using, performing, or demonstrating.

For example, you may really enjoy customer service. Therefore, you should think carefully about why you like customer service. You may want to ask yourself the following questions:

What does quality customer service mean to you?
What makes you motivated about customer service?
What kind of career do you want in customer service?
What skills are necessary to be good at customer service?
What do you like most about customer service?

So, now let's get back to Bob, Sally, and Vince; how will they address their respective inventory of professional attributes?

Tuesday, January 13th – As they share warm buttermilk biscuits and coffee for brunch at the kitchen table, Bob and Mary start talking about Bob's work responsibilities over the past several years. As Bob talks, Mary takes copious notes. Eventually, they have enough information to begin itemizing and prioritizing Bob's strengths, weaknesses, skills, knowledge, expertise, as well as likes and dislikes.

Although Mary is a stay-at-home mom, she has a few friends who work in human resources/recruiting roles. Mary is knowledgeable about what prospective employers seek in potential job candidates. This knowledge and information comes in handy, as the next step for Bob is to prepare a well-written resume. The resume should effectively present his key strengths, skills, accomplishments, and achievements.

As a talented and knowledgeable customer service manager, Sally never took the time to document her notable accomplishments. In fact, Sally does not have a resume, because she thought her job at the company was as close to permanent as possible. However, she now knows a resume is critical to continuing her work life journey. But, Sally is concerned about how to prepare her resume. The time has come for her to seek help – and from unlikely sources like Joe the coffee shop owner.

———◉———

Wednesday, January 14th – Sally visits the coffee shop as she has done so many times before. As always, Joe personally greets one of his favorite customers. Soon Sally and Joe are talking about her jobless situation. Joe listens carefully as Sally talks about her layoff. Suddenly, Joe interrupts Sally, "Don't worry, everything will work out, and I am going to help you." Sally smiles, but wonders how Joe can help her.

First, Joe reminds Sally she has a great personality and how good she is with people. Second, Joe reminds Sally he was a successful corporate executive for many years before becoming an entrepreneur. Therefore, Joe understands the people management process – from recruiting, evaluating, and hiring candidates to helping employees manage their careers.

Joe tells Sally, "There is more to Sally I know than just a resume. What we need to do is work on preparing you for your next job. And, we will begin by meeting here in the coffee shop every day for the next two weeks," he says. "We will work together, step by step, on your job search process, from writing a good resume to interview preparation." Joe starts the process by giving Sally some homework. She needs to write about her strengths, weaknesses, knowledge, skills, accomplishments, and achievements, as well as her likes and dislikes.

The goal, of course, is to capture this information in the format of a well-written resume. However, Joe is going beyond the resume and helping Sally with her "visual and verbal resume" – the job interview. "So, let's take this one step at a time," says Joe. "I would like you to visit this coffee shop every day at 10 a.m. for the next two weeks. We are going to talk in detail about your recent job, the key responsibilities, challenges, and successes."

From there, Joe plans to develop a roadmap – a series of activities – for Sally to complete. This roadmap will reveal her true experiences and talents. Ultimately, Joe is helping Sally document her inventory of personal attributes. This information will help her develop a personal branding message and author a well-written resume. In turn, Sally hopes to launch an effective job search, and prepare herself to achieve success in the interview process.

Wednesday evening, January 14th – Vince calls some of his buddies to meet at the local pub. As they all gather around the pool table, Vince talks about his layoff situation. Vince really appreciates and values his friendships. While Vince remains bitter about the layoff, his friends quickly offer words of encouragement and support. These guys will do anything for each other. Vince realizes his friends may know people who are looking for skilled laborers or perhaps even other people who may be seeking some extra help.

Personal Challenge:

What is your inventory of personal attributes?

How often do you review your inventory of personal attributes?

Where can you improve?

What actions are your taking to improve?

Craft Your Personal Branding Message

As you progress through the work life journey, it is often easy to lose sight of the knowledge, expertise, and abilities you have developed over time. Think about the last time someone said to you, "Tell me about yourself." You may have been asked such a question during a job interview, or perhaps during a conversation with a colleague or a chance meeting with someone in the elevator. How did you respond to the "tell me about yourself" question? It is one of the most challenging and stressful questions to answer.

What is the ideal response?

What information should be included?

What is the appropriate response length?

You should develop the ability to articulate your interests, knowledge, experiences, and skills in a quick and confident manner. **One proven method to accomplish this task is to develop your personal branding message – the 10th practical concept to understand and apply in the evolution of your work life journey.** Over time, you acquire knowledge and abilities to accomplish activities and achieve goals. However, you do not always think about how to effectively summarize your personal brand until you are forced to do so – like after a layoff.

The personal branding message informs people about your knowledge and talent in 90 seconds or less. In other words, the personal branding message is a classic sales or elevator pitch. However, the message is not about a specific product or service but instead about your knowledge, expertise, skills, accomplishments, and future job pursuits. In other words, your personal branding message communicates the value your brand has to offer. Therefore, you should take your time to craft a well-developed personal branding message.

There are six basic elements for a personal branding message:

1. Your name.
2. A brief description of your most recent work experience (including company name, title, and key responsibilities).
3. A brief summary of your other work experiences, achievements, or accomplishments (as applicable).
4. A brief explanation for leaving your most recent employer.
5. Your top two or three personal attributes.
6. Finally, a discussion of the next pursuit in your work life journey.

Once you create a personal branding message, the next step is to develop the ability to share your message with others. You may need your personal branding message in an interview, networking situation or daily interaction with others in your network of contacts. Your personal branding message is also useful for those chance meetings with someone in an elevator, retail store or coffee shop. Your personal branding message offers your friends, colleagues and other contacts to gain a quick understanding about what you know, what you want to do and what you have to offer.

So, now let's get back to Bob, Sally, and Vince; how will they develop their own personal branding message?

Thursday, January 15th – Sally meets Joe at the coffee shop as scheduled. Today, Joe works with Sally to create her personal branding message. The personal branding message will help her establish meaningful contacts and conversations in her active job search. Joe understands the enormous value behind being ready to share your personal branding message with others in your network. In a highly demanding and competitive global economy, the personal branding message can help you effectively sell your knowledge and abilities quickly and confidently. Joe asks Sally a series of questions, which allows them to develop an appropriate personal branding message as shown in Figure 1.

Figure 1 – Sally's Personal Branding Message

"Hi, my name is Sally, and I was a Customer Service Manager for Acme Manufacturing Corporation. I was responsible for providing quality service for a large portfolio of customers. Due to economic conditions, the company decided to implement a workforce reduction program. I have exceptional customer service skills; any many customers gave me the highest service ratings for the past three years. I am seeking a similar role within organization seeking to leverage my exceptional capabilities.

Friday, January 16th – Bob and Mary continue discussing Bob's roles and responsibilities over the last several years. During their conversation, Bob begins to draft a short personal branding message (as shown in Figure 2) designed to effectively "summarize" his key strengths, accomplishments, and plan for the immediate future. Bob has already started to reach out to his friends and business colleagues. Therefore, Bob wants to be prepared for such networking connections or meetings by being able to clearly articulate his background and plan for the future.

Figure 2 – Bob's Personal Branding Message

"Hi, my name is Bob, and I was recently an Accounting Supervisor for Acme Manufacturing Corporation. I am a CPA with in-depth experience in monthly financial close, corporate tax, audit, and special projects. Due to current economic conditions, the company implemented a work force reduction program. I have been recognized multiple times for my accounting expertise. I am seeking similar role within a reputable organization."

Vince also thinks about his personal branding message. He wants to express his passion for performing quality work and commitment to excellence. Additionally, Vince is a dedicated worker who understands the meaning behind the saying "an honest day's pay for an honest day's work." Some may say Vince has old-fashioned values and beliefs. However, those values and beliefs are timeless, and everyone should aspire to have such values and beliefs. Figure 3 illustrates Vince's personal branding message.

Figure 3 – Vince's Personal Branding Message

> "Hello, my name is Vince, and I was recently a Senior Assembler for Acme Manufacturing Corporation. Unfortunately, the company fell on hard times during this economy, and many good people were recently laid off. I offer a strong work ethic and passion for doing quality work. I would like to join a company that will give me a chance to prove my worth every day, while allowing me the opportunity to make a difference in the manufacturing process of a local manufacturing company."

Remember, you have one chance to make a positive and memorable first impression. The personal branding message offers an opportunity to advertise your brand before the interview even begins.

Personal Challenge:

What is your personal branding message?

How long is your personal branding message?

How often do you practice your personal branding message?

What do others say about your personal branding message?

Write that Resume

The **11th practical concept to follow in the evolution of your work life journey is to prepare a well-written and action-oriented resume presenting you as the ideal candidate for the job.** An effective resume is a summary of your accomplishments and achievements. It is also a snapshot of your work experience and educational credentials. More importantly, the resume is a one or two-page marketing document, which offers prospective employers a good starting point as to why you are a worthy candidate for the job. However, the resume itself does not guarantee an offer for employment. Rather, the resume is a call to action for prospective employers to take the next step in the recruiting process – inviting you for an interview.

Now, regardless of whether you already have a resume or not, it is always wise to consider the **12th practical concept in your work life journey – identify resources to help you prepare an effective, well-written resume.** These resources can be your friends, family members, co-workers, colleagues, or career coaches/mentors. Other reference resources include the Internet, books and articles discussing resume preparation. There are also outplacement organizations, as well as customized career coaching. However, keep in mind, there may be fees for these services.

The resume is the first opportunity to capture a prospective employer's attention to your personal attributes and accomplishments. And, in today's highly volatile and uncertain economy, you owe it yourself to seek every available advantage. The ability to share your accomplishments in a clear and concise manner is critical. In fact, this can be the difference between being invited to an interview and being cast aside for other more presentable and qualified candidates.

The resume is one the most important documents in your work life journey. You are the writer, director and producer of the resume and your image. Just as a book can be the primer for a motion picture, the resume can highlight your value to a prospective employer. Regardless of where you are in the work life journey, the concept of writing a resume can also be a daunting challenge for even the most experienced and articulate person.

Writing a resume is a three-phase process. The first phase is *organizing* – gathering information about your qualifications, employment history and educational background. Start with a blank sheet of paper, or a simple index card, for each employer in your work history and each academic institution or training organization attended.

For each employer, list the following information:

- Actual dates of employment (presented in years, for example 1999 – 2003).
- Key roles and responsibilities.
- Major contributions, accomplishments, achievements, or awards.

Next, present your educational or training experience and accomplishments. The name of the institution and degree program or name of training program is sufficient. It is not necessary to indicate when you attended school or participated in the training program. Phase one should also include a comprehensive inventory of personal attributes, which will come in handy for the "summary of strengths" or "highlights of qualifications" section of the resume. This is the first section a prospective employer will see after your name and contact information at the top of the resume. Therefore, you owe it to yourself to think carefully about the following:

- Industry knowledge (for example, manufacturing)

- Functional experience (for example, accounts payable)
- Subject matter expertise (for example, international financial reporting standards)
- Technical abilities (for example – working with an enterprise resource planning or ERP system).

The second phase of the resume writing process is *drafting*. Once you have gathered your resume information, the next step is to seek alignment between this information and the job you want. For this reason, your resume should also allow for customization – the ability to reorganize and rephrase key information to address specific job requirements. The second phase of resume writing is also challenging because of the amount of information available to start drafting key sections of the resume:

- *Header* – section dedicated to listing your name, address, and contact information.
- *Professional Objective* – typically used by recent college graduates or those people with less than three years of professional experience.
- *Summary of Qualifications* – commonly used by people with a minimum of three years experience, where key skills, knowledge, expertise, abilities are listed to give the resume reader an immediate idea of the candidate's strengths and expertise. This section also can be referred to as the "Highlights of Qualifications."
- *Work Experience* – chronological listing of current and previous employment experiences including name of employer, location, title, dates of employment and key accomplishments and activities/responsibilities.
- *Education* – summary of academic credentials and/or training experience.

Of course, the resume content must be complete, accurate, honest, and free of any errors (typos or misspelled words). It is also important to note that "References Available upon Request" is no longer necessary on the resume, as it is widely accepted people have references if necessary.

The third, and final, phase of resume writing is *editing*. While you may think editing is about checking spelling, grammar and punctuation, the far more difficult aspect of editing is reviewing the resume content. In other words, the challenge is to determine whether you have presented your personal brand as effectively as possible. Some people like to tell stories and provide more detail than is necessary. Resumes should not exceed one page in length unless you have a lengthy employment history. Even then, you should have other trusted friends or colleagues review your resume. In the end, be ruthless in your editing or ask others for their genuine critique.

You want to be brief and brilliant with your resume. In other words, think less is more. One page is more than enough to showcase your talent or personal brand. However, as you accumulate more experience, 10 or more years, you may need a two-page resume to articulate the breadth and depth of your knowledge, experience, and expertise. Remember, a prospective employer may have 30 seconds or less to look over or just glance at a resume, so the concept of grabbing the reader's attention is critical.

As you write your resume, you will discover drafting a resume is often an iterative process. You may find yourself with multiple versions before you come up with the finished product. Content accuracy and honesty are critical, as well as style and the use of action verbs to demonstrate your knowledge, skills, expertise, and accomplishments. Table 4 offers some commonly used action verbs.

Table 4 – Action-Oriented Verbs

Analyzed	Evaluated	Performed
Advised	Identified	Provided
Created	Managed	Reviewed
Directed	Organized	Implemented

There are many more action verbs available. A thesaurus is a good reference tool to use for identifying action-oriented verbs to appropriately describe your knowledge, skills, expertise, and accomplishments. While the content of a resume is critical, the overall appearance must also convey a professional image. Therefore, the following basic resume formatting guidelines are widely accepted:

- Use either an Arial or Times Roman font – size 10-point or 11-point.
- Maintain clear 1-inch margins – top, bottom, left, and right.
- Use simple bullets to state key roles, responsibilities, and achievements/accomplishments for each employer.
- Use boldface words to distinguish major sections of the resume.
- Use keywords relating to words or terminology included in the job description (as applicable).
- Make the resume easy to read and understand, using simple words and appropriate line spacing.
- Avoid using graphics to spice up the resume, except for various artistic or graphic design vocations, where creativity may be more appropriate.

The Internet offers a convenient and practical way to research resume styles. The key is to use a style appropriate for the job you want to pursue. For business jobs, such as those in accounting, finance, marketing or human resources, the classic chronological style is widely accepted. For other occupations, such as graphic design, fashion merchandising or Internet-based jobs, a more creative approach may also work well. In fact, for these types of job opportunities, it is common to have other materials as part of your resume portfolio. Examples of your creative work including drawings, designs, or photographs may be required to determine your candidacy for the job.

Figure 4 illustrates a typical chronological resume, which includes the major resume sections presenting the candidate's key strengths or qualifications, accomplishments, and technical/educational history. The chronological resume lists your talents, experience, and educational history in logical order over a period of time. Most resume experts and industry professionals suggest the resume should include vital information over the past 10 years. Prospective employers want to know more about your recent work experience, as opposed to jobs you held more than 10 years ago.

From recent college graduates to entry-level professionals and those in middle management, the chronological resume offers a quick synopsis of practical experience and academic history. The work life journey includes milestones and accomplishments prospective employers want to learn more about. The goal of the resume is simple: grab the attention of the prospective employer and get an invitation to interview for the job. From there, your verbal skills should articulate the merits of your resume, coupled with your passion for the job and the future.

In the end, your resume should be a well-written and professional-looking document. It should convey your personal brand in a clear, concise, coherent, and convincing manner.

Figure 4 – Chronological Resume

JOHN SMITH
CPA, CIA

123 Sample Lane
Newtown, IL 60656

Cell: 312-555-5555
JohnSmith@yourmail.com

HIGHLIGHTS OF QUALIFICATIONS

A focused audit practitioner with 15 years of progressive experience spanning multiple industries including management consulting specializing in internal audit and regulatory compliance services. Demonstrated knowledge, skills and abilities include:

- American Recovery & Reinvestment Act (ARRA)
- Sarbanes-Oxley (SOX) – Section 404
- Active CIA; BS in Accounting (Roosevelt)
- Project management and leadership

PROFESSIONAL EXPERIENCE

Acme Consulting, LLC
Chicago, IL
Engagement Manager
2012 – Present
Accomplishments, achievements, and subject matter expertise
- Consistently achieved outstanding client service ratings, which led to a $1.2M increase in revenue from new and existing clients in my portfolio.
- Recipient of the firm's Exceptional Client Service Award for the past three consecutive years.
- Assisted clients achieve a combined $18.6M in cost reduction in 2023 through several key strategic sourcing and process improvement engagements.
Internal controls, risk management, and regulatory compliance (SOX section 404)
- Lead management consultant for a SOX-404 project at a $3 billion global manufacturing client with operating entities in the North America, Europe, Latin America, and Asia/Pacific regions.
- Oversee an internal controls assessment for a $2 billion client in the agricultural industry.

Local Audit Services
Chicago, IL
Consultant
2010 – 2012
- Member of a consulting team that assisted an international financial services organization develop and implement a strategic sourcing initiative that uncovered opportunities to reduce corporate-wide consulting expenditures by 15%, or $8.2M, annually across North America.
- Assisted partners develop and launch the Business Risk Strategy Consulting (BRSC) practice.
- Participated in client meetings to understand and document the overall internal and external risk management framework and approach within the client organizations.

EDUCATION

Certified Public Accountant (CPA)
Certified Internal Auditor (CIA)

Roosevelt University
Chicago, IL
BS – Bachelor of Science in Accounting

One more comment about your resume. You should save the electronic version of your resume using a simple naming convention (first and last name, date, as well as year and version number). For example, JamesSmith-2011 v1.doc (assuming you use MS Word for writing documents). You should avoid using catchy names for your resume unless the job opportunity requires you to demonstrate your creative abilities. Even then, I recommend using a simple and effective naming convention so recruiters can immediately associate with the person and the resume. A catchy or otherwise creative resume name does not allow a recruiter to search for your resume in a quick and efficient manner.

You should use the simple naming convention regardless of how often you update or change your resume. Remember, you may need to customize your resume for specific job opportunities. Therefore, you may need to save multiple versions of your resume for easy future reference. I have resumes customized for different industries such as government and management consulting.

Of course, writing and saving the resume is one thing. Reviewing it and keeping it current is another matter. I review my resume at least once a quarter, or a minimum of four times per year. For you, it may make sense to review your resume once or twice a year. Regardless of the review frequency, the point is to review your resume periodically to ensure your work experiences, achievements and educational credentials are current and appropriately reflect your personal brand and accomplishments to date.

I also have a short list of trusted colleagues who review my resume upon request. Remember, the time people devote to reviewing and editing your resume is valuable. So, be sincere in your request for resume review. You should always express your sincere appreciation for any support/assistance you receive from family, friends, and colleagues.

⎯⎯◉⎯⎯

So, now let's get back to Bob, Sally, and Vince; how will they address the importance of having a well-written resume to present their personal brand?

Monday, January 19th – Bob has a draft resume, but he wonders if it's effective. Therefore, Bob does something that seems trivial at the time but proves to be critical. Bob e-mails his resume to three trusted friends, Gary, Steven, and David, for their comments and constructive criticism. A few days later, Bob receives feedback from his buddies identifying areas for improvement.

Gary suggests Bob use more action-oriented verbs. Steven finds grammar and punctuation errors. David, on the other hand, challenges Bob to better articulate his key accomplishments in his most recent position. Bob realizes as writer, director, and producer of his resume, it is easy for him to overlook the errors and suggestions his friends identify. Thankful to his friends for their assistance, Bob sends a sincere thank you e-mail to each of them for their time and effort. The collaborative effort helps Bob create a much-improved resume for the job search ahead.

⸻⬤⸻

Are you required to have others review your resume before you start applying for jobs? Of course not, but it is strongly recommended to ensure you avoid any mistakes or errors. Remember, the resume is a particularly important document, which communicates the personal brand known as you. I have yet to meet anyone who can catch every mistake on his or her own resume. A second pair of eyes almost always reveals things the resume author does not see.

Once Bob's resume is final, he quickly starts responding to open job advertisements using multiple methods including the Internet, friends and colleagues, professional associations, and the college career center. When looking to make a transition in your work life journey, it is wise to pursue multiple methods to identify suitable job opportunities. The Internet, in particular, provides a wide array of avenues to seek jobs relevant to your inventory of personal attributes.

In fact, the Internet provides the opportunity to upload your resume for prospective employers to view at any given time. This means you search for jobs yourself, but prospective employers can see you are looking as well. Of course, relationships remain the best way to get your personal brand noticed for potential opportunities. Otherwise, you are at the mercy of a numbers game, one of many candidates pursuing the same job through the lens of the corporate human resources function.

———◦———

Thursday, January 22nd – Sally, with a lot of help from Joe, has a resume ready for distribution. However, the key for Sally is to focus the job search to identify the ideal opportunities to effectively use her strengths toward achieving future success. Many people fail to understand that looking for the next step in the work life journey is a lot like having a full-time job. Hence, the need for a positive, focused attitude at all times.

———◦———

Having a well-written resume is one thing, but being able to articulate your personal brand to others verbally is another matter. So, Sally must also work on her communication, persuasion, and presentation skills. Do you actively work on your communication, persuasion, and presentation skills? I said this before, but I will say it again: communication is the lifeline of every personal and business relationship. It is absolutely true. Your ability to effectively reach your audience is the key to getting your message heard, believed, and acted upon.

There is no scientific method, formula, or secret to improving your communication skills. Rather, the **13th practical concept to remember in your work life journey is developing a disciplined approach to continuous professional development.** You communicate every day, so you should work every day to improve your ability to communicate – not just when a layoff occurs.

Personal Challenge:

Do you have a resume?

When was the last time you reviewed your resume?

How often do you review your resume?

Who else reviews your resume?

What do others say about your resume?

Pursue Multiple Channels for Your Job Search

It is common to apply to as many opportunities as possible after a layoff. However, it is critical to identify the attributes of a job relevant to your abilities and career interests. Once you identify these job attributes, it is wise to explore and pursue several channels in the job search. Here is a list of the commonly used channels in the job search process:

- Networking activities (e.g., relationships with family, friends, and colleagues).
- Social networking websites such as LinkedIn, Facebook, and Twitter, which can greatly expand your network of contacts and uncover potential job leads.
- Recruiting firms and executive search firms that work directly with companies to find qualified candidates for jobs within their client organizations.
- Job postings on company websites.
- Job postings on Internet job boards (e.g., CareerBuilder.com, Monster.com, Glassdoor.com, Indeed.com, and many others).
- Career centers at academic institutions (e.g., junior colleges and four-year universities).
- Job postings in publications (i.e., newspapers, trade journals, magazines).

Among the commonly used job search channels, networking offers the highest success rate. *Studies have shown up to 70% of jobs are obtained through networking.* The reason is simple – hiring managers are more likely to hire candidates they know or have worked with as opposed to candidates they do not know. Networking is by far the *most recommended* job search channel to fully explore – not just when you are in transition after a layoff but also when you are contemplating a career move from your current job.

Social networking websites such LinkedIn.com offer another good, practical means to get your personal brand noticed in the job market. While social networking offers you the opportunity to connect with those you know or would like to know, these websites also provide a platform to present your knowledge, skills, and specific expertise. When you are looking for the next chapter in your work life journey, you need to use every available tool to communicate your personal brand.

Search firms and executive recruiters offer another vehicle to uncover possible opportunities to further explore. These channels work with the companies looking to hire qualified candidates for open jobs – or sometimes jobs which are not yet announced or posted on any job search channel, the so called "hidden job market." However, there are many search firms and executive recruiters in the marketplace. Once again, you should do your homework before working with a search firm or executive recruiter to better understand the services they have to offer. In addition, you want to know how the search firm plans to market your background and skills to prospective employers and if fees are required for their services.

Company websites offer another excellent job search channel. The concept here is simple – you can view available job openings within prospective companies and apply for such opportunities on the company website. Most companies allow you to attach or upload your resume in response to job openings by creating an online job search account. All you need is a valid e-mail address to successfully create an online user ID and password. This direct application process allows company Human Resources departments to capture your resume quickly and conveniently without any third-party involvement. Best of all, this approach is free.

A couple of the more widely used online job search channels are CareerBuilder.com and Monster.com. These powerful job search databases have job listings across all occupations in all geographies – national and international. However, like the many other job boards available, they also represent the classic "numbers game," since so many people may be applying to open jobs. Remember also to consider relevant job opportunities on the actual websites of those companies you find interesting. For example, you can create a job profile account with specific companies in industries you like. While a personal job search account offers no guarantee of getting the job, it does offer an efficient method to make prospective employers aware of you.

As the saying goes, "never put all your eggs in one basket" – or in this case just one job search channel. Rather, take advantage of several job search channels simultaneously. Consider exploring, and applying for, opportunities matching your search criteria across different job search channels. For example, think about industries and companies you would want to work for based on your inventory of personal attributes. The Internet is a powerful tool for doing this. It allows you to conduct research on industry information, as well as explore job opportunities aligned with your interests and inventory of personal attributes.

Career centers at academic institutions, preferably those you attended, also offer a job database for you to explore. Again, this job search channel is like job boards, since many applicants may respond to the same job opening. However, career centers can also offer other services helpful in your job search – for example resume review, interview preparation, and career counseling services.

Among the job search channels, job postings in publications like newspapers or trade magazines are no longer the preferred method.

The Internet and e-mail have rendered this traditional job search method obsolete.

Personal Challenge:

What job search are you using?

What job search channels are you not using? Why?

Network, Network, and Network Some More

Let's face it; there is no joy in being laid off. And, as I said before, the emotions surrounding a layoff can cover the entire spectrum of feelings, from anger to tears. The bottom line is you must gain control of your emotions so you can move forward. A common reaction to a layoff is to keep quiet and not talk about what has happened. I cannot emphasize enough how wrong it is to just keep quiet and not talk about the layoff. There is no benefit from keeping the layoff a secret. None, absolutely none. This points to the **14th practical concept in addressing your work life journey – tell everyone you know about your layoff, including family, friends, and colleagues.** You never know who will have a lead, a referral or other information to help you gain focus or identify the next step in your work life journey.

Before you begin to inform anyone about your layoff situation, understand the **15th practical concept in the work life journey – start the networking process by creating a list of everyone you love, know, work with, spend time with or meet occasionally.** You will be surprised how many people you interact with on some level, either daily or just once in awhile. However, you should understand your network of contacts is important throughout your life, not just when a layoff occurs. In other words, you should try to stay connected with people in your network regardless of where you are in the work life journey.

Once you have prepared your list, the next step is to follow the **16th practical concept in the work life journey – identify the primary and secondary contacts on your list.** Primary contacts are those who know you well and with whom you interact with on a regular basis. Secondary contacts are people you associate with occasionally or know because of your primary contacts. However, you should also note who on your primary and secondary lists of contacts is, or maybe, able to help you in your job search. Not everyone on the list may be able to assist you or want to.

So, tell everyone you know on your primary and secondary contact lists about your layoff in a practical and respectful manner. You should also demonstrate your proactive, positive attitude toward overcoming your layoff. A good place to start talking about your layoff is with family members, who can help you – financially or otherwise. Second, tell your friends, who may in turn tell their friends.

Tell your co-workers and other professional colleagues, who in turn may inform their business associates about your situation and interests. A quick, effective way to ensure you reach out to as many people as possible is to maintain a list of contacts. You can use a notebook or your personal computer to manage your contact list. The key is to create the list and manage it from time to time.

You have many alternatives to explore and expand your network of contacts. While face-to-face meetings and chance interactions are common networking opportunities, the Internet has become a networking phenomenon. Social media websites such as Facebook, Twitter, and LinkedIn offer convenient and practical opportunities to stay in touch with your network of contacts. These websites also provide the ability to seek and establish new contacts around the world.

Stop and think for a moment about all the people you come across in the daily course of your life. These "chance" interactions may not offer immediate leads in your work life journey. However, these mere acquaintances can lead to lasting relationships. And sometimes, these relationships can lead to potential opportunities you would not have otherwise uncovered without having the initial chance encounter on the bus or train.

⎯⎯⎯◉⎯⎯⎯

Several years ago, my best friend, Jack, was looking for a job in the finance field. At the same time Ken, another good friend, was looking for a junior level accountant to join his team. Based on my relationship with Ken, and the conversation we had during lunch, I began to talk about Jack and his skills and career interests. Ken asked me to forward him a copy of Jack's resume. The rest, as they say, is history. Jack was invited for an interview and eventually was hired for the job and went on to become an assistant vice president. In fact, Jack continues to achieve greater success in his professional journey due in large part to his networking efforts.

My colleague Melissa is a more recent example of how networking can be a remarkably effective and powerful job search method. Melissa was looking for a new job, as her existing job no longer offered much of a career progression. As Melissa was looking and networking, a friend of hers called about a job opportunity within the company's accounting department. After discussing the job and related responsibilities, Melissa decided to submit a resume through her friend as a referral candidate. Melissa was contacted the very next day by the company human resources manager. Soon thereafter, Melissa interviewed for the job with the hiring manager. And, two days later Melissa received a verbal job offer. Wow! Now that is what I call an expedited job search.

In an otherwise chaotic real world, the job search process often takes longer than just two days. Remember, the job search process is more like a marathon race than a quick sprint to the finish line. The point is that you should never underestimate the profound impact networking and relationships can have on your work life journey.

***

You may go to church on a regular basis, volunteer in your community, attend social networking clubs, or perhaps participate in local bowling leagues or fantasy sports leagues. These activities present opportunities to expand your network of contacts. You never know when a simple introduction or small conversation can lead to something more. Think about the last time you went to the local mall, theater, bank, or grocery store. It may not happen often, but you never know when a chance meeting can turn into a brief discussion or possibly a new contact or relationship in your personal network.

I understand it is not comfortable to talk about your layoff. But you must overcome the anger, embarrassment, denial, and any other emotion or thought preventing you from talking about it. *Remember to understand the power, and need, behind having a positive attitude.* Many people simply do not realize it takes the same amount of energy to have a positive attitude as it does to express a negative attitude. Put another way, people would rather associate with a positive-minded person than one who is engulfed in negativity or self-pity.

Anyone can network. Let me say it again, anyone can network. You do not need a special skill. All you need is the desire to meet people without feeling awkward or experiencing fear. As in the case of public speaking, it takes discipline and practice to improve your networking efforts. The more people you meet, the more chances you have to practice your personal branding message.

The idea is not to memorize your personal branding message. Rather, become consistent in articulating the primary theme and key points of your message. People are intelligent enough to know when you simply recite a message, as opposed to when you are sharing a genuine description of your background, strengths, and job search.

Never underestimate the power of networking. Visit the career development department at local junior colleges or universities (particularly those you have some affiliation with). Effective networking enables you to inform others, including prospective employers, about your experience, knowledge, skills, and job search. Get the word out to as many people as possible.

To succeed at networking, you must know and communicate your strengths and interests – your personal branding message. Networking is not a one-time effort or event. Rather, networking should be a continuous activity, regardless of whether you are currently employed or not. Throughout your work life journey, you can interface and collaborate with other people with diverse backgrounds and experiences.

As you inform people in your network about your layoff, begin taking time to meet with as many of the people in your network as possible – particularly those you believe can offer relevant advice or assistance in your job search. Remember to respect their time. Be willing to meet your contacts according to their schedules. I like to meet at the local coffee shop to reconnect with people in my network. However, you could accomplish the same objective over the phone if you or your network contacts are short on time.

This brings me to the **17th practical concept to understand in your work life journey: self-discipline. Stay in touch with the trusted people on your network contact list (family, friends, and colleagues) on a consistent basis.** Remember, communication is the lifeline of every business and personal relationship. I make it a priority to stay connected with trusted friends and colleagues in my professional network every quarter.

There is a saying, "no one who has friends is ever a failure." Put differently, the work life journey is not a solo act. Rather, the journey, if navigated effectively, includes interaction and collaboration with many people – family, friends, co-workers, colleagues, and acquaintances. Such interaction and collaboration can provide other opportunities, which in turn can yield more opportunities on the path to work life fulfillment.

Additional Tools for More Effective Networking

Another key tool you can use in the networking process is a *handbill document*, which is an abbreviated version of your resume. The handbill is also referred to as a networking brief. While the resume provides details about skills, employment history, and educational background, the handbill is designed to address five basic concepts.

- *Who I am...* "an accomplished former chief executive officer with extensive experience leading medium-sized organizations in the banking and financial services industries."
- *How I can add value...*"proven track record managing a $35 million book of business, while achieving president's club status for three consecutive years."
- *What I am looking for...*"a leadership position within the finance function of a Fortune 500 company in the health care or pharmaceutical industries."
- *Target industries and companies of interest*
- *Positions of interest* (e.g., staff accountant)

The handbill is designed to provide brief descriptions of your talents, expertise and accomplishments across key business functions or activities. In other words, the handbill is a formal way to present your inventory of personal attributes. For example, you may have achieved success in business development (e.g., generated significant sales over a period of time) or expertise in process improvement, which led to significant cost savings. Like the resume, the handbill includes your name, address, and contact information. The handbill is useful at networking events, where people can quickly learn more about your skills, interests, and work life pursuits (i.e., ideal job, ideal employer). You can search the word "handbill" on the Internet to obtain more information.

Another useful tool for enhancing your networking efforts is a *personal business card*. There are many designs and styles of business cards, so take some time to think about how you want to market your personal brand and image. For example, if the target profession is accounting or finance, go with a conservative look. On the other hand, if graphic design is your area of interest or expertise, a more creative design/style may be more appropriate.

The personal business card can be either horizontal or vertical in format, depending on personal preference. Although the vertical format is unique, most business cards use the traditional horizontal layout. Use a good quality card stock for either format. As for the content on the personal business card, the following basics are essential:

- Name
- Educational credentials (e.g., BS, MS, MBA, PhD)
- Professional certifications (e.g., CPA, PMP)
- Areas of expertise
- Phone information (e.g., mobile, home/office)
- E-mail address
- Social media website (such as LinkedIn, Facebook, or Twitter)

The personal business card, as shown in Figure 3, is a simple way to provide your personal brand information to others at networking events. In addition, the personal business card offers a convenient way to distribute your personal brand without having to carry lots of paper (i.e., copies of your resume or handbill).

Figure 5 – Personal Business Card Example

Jennifer Jones
CPA MBA

Accounting/Finance
Professional

Areas of Expertise
Monthly Financial Close
Management Reporting
Budgeting
SAP and Hyperion

Contact Information

312-555-5555
jjones@notmail.com
LinkedIn Profile

A quick Internet search will reveal multiple sources to help you create your personal business card. The actual resume is critical for job fair events. However, it never hurts to have the personal business card to handout. Whether the event is networking oriented or a job fair, you should be ready to articulate your personal branding message.

Personal Challenge:

Do you have a handbill document or personal business card?

When did you last review your handbill document or personal business card?

What do others say about your handbill document and personal business card?

Understand the C.H.A.R.M. factor

Over the years I have met, and in many cases collaborated with, many people from all walks of life, particularly during the job search process. If there is one concept to effectively describe a successful job search, it is what I call **"the C.H.A.R.M. factor" – the 18th practical concept to understand in the work life journey.**

C is for confidence – before others can believe in you, you must believe in yourself.

H is for habits – good habits require good discipline.

A is for attitude – always project a positive attitude.

R is for respect – treat others as you want them to treat you.

M is for motivation – demonstrate energy and commitment to achieve success.

Table 5 – Assessing Your C.H.A.R.M. Factor

C	Confidence	1 2 3 4 5
H	Habits	1 2 3 4 5
A	Attitude	1 2 3 4 5
R	Respect	1 2 3 4 5
M	Motivation	1 2 3 4 5

Table 5 illustrates a simple assessment you can take to determine your C.H.A.R.M. factor. Just circle the most appropriate response to each category, where 1 is weak and 5 represents strong. Remember, there is no right or wrong answer, so be honest.

Now, add up the numerical values for each response and divide the total by five. This represents your C.H.A.R.M. factor. A score of 0 – 3 suggests there is room for improvement. A score of 4 – 5 suggests a healthy C.H.A.R.M. factor. Regardless of your score, the key is to work on your C.H.A.R.M. factor every day. A daily focus requires good fundamental discipline. This is not hard, but it does take effort on your part.

Think about those people you consider highly successful. How do you think those people rate according to the C.H.A.R.M. factor? The fact is the C.H.A.R.M. factor is not an inherited attribute. Rather, the C.H.A.R.M. factor evolves over the work life journey. More importantly, the C.H.A.R.M. factor is about fundamental discipline – the willingness to learn and understand the impact of confidence, habits, attitude, respect, and motivation on your work life journey.

> **Personal Challenge:**
>
> What is your C.H.A.R.M. factor?
>
> How can you improve your C.H.A.R.M. factor?

No Second Chance for a First Impression

Just as the resume describes you as the ideal personal brand in writing, the interview is the opportunity to demonstrate your knowledge and inventory of personal attributes. While technical knowledge and experience are important, many experts say being articulate is essential in a highly competitive marketplace. This leads me to the **19th practical concept to understand in your work life journey – there is no such thing as a second chance to make a good first impression, so be ready and prepared.**

Like anything you have learned in the past, such as swimming, reading, or managing projects, being effective in interviews is an acquired skill you can develop with practice. I do not believe in the perfect interview. Rather, I believe what my father has told me throughout my life – believe in yourself. You should make a commitment to do the best you can, but without expecting a perfect fit every time.

While it is always appropriate to have dreams and goals, never lose sight of what you need to do to achieve those dreams and goals. And, if you do not fulfill a dream or achieve a desired goal, it is not the end of the world. Be true to yourself, and then give it your best shot and let the results follow. Remember, there are no guarantees in this journey called life. In other words, you cannot control external factors such as hiring decisions. However, you can, and should, take control of your personal efforts to be able to achieve success – like performing well during an interview and potentially getting a job offer.

Of all my previous job pursuits, one stands out. I had just completed my second master's degree in communication from Northwestern University and was looking to get back into the workforce after a two-year absence. That's right. I had gone back to graduate school without holding a steady job. And, to make matters even more complicated, I found myself in a lot of student debt...again!

After graduation, I received a call from an executive recruiter. He was conducting a search for manager level position at a technology company located in San Francisco. The job, however, was in Chicago supporting the Central Region of the country. At first, I did not believe I was the ideal fit for the job. However, upon further discussion with the recruiter regarding my skills, knowledge, and professional interests, I agreed to meet with the regional vice president and members of his team.

I knew I had to prepare thoroughly for three local interviews. This meant I had to learn as much about the company as possible. The preparation was critical, as I was then invited to interview with members of the senior management team in San Francisco. While I was successful in getting the job offer, the point of my story is that I made a commitment to prepare for several interviews before the hiring decision was made.

In my case, the interview process involved several interview methods: one-on-one; multi-person; and a panel. First, I interviewed with the executive recruiter. Next, I had an office visit with the local office of the company, which entailed three separate interviews. Finally, I experienced a panel interview with several members of the senior management team.

———◉———

The interview process for job opportunities may not involve multiple interview methods. However, it is always a good practice to prepare for the unexpected. In other words, an interview may start as a one-on-one discussion over the phone and then evolve into an interview "marathon" involving multiple people in the company. And, some interviewers may be direct colleagues of the position, while other interviewers may be peers who have an indirect relationship to the position.

So, you may be asking, exactly how did I prepare for a multi-method interview process? First, I was told I would have multiple interviews with people in the local office. If the local office visit went well, the company would fly me to San Francisco for meetings with members of the senior management team. Second, I prepared myself for distinct types of interviews, which brings me to the **20th practical concept to remember in the work life journey – prepare for the three categories of interview questions: technical, behavioral, and "think on your feet" questions.**

Technical questions are asked to determine your level of subject matter expertise in a function, process, activity, or concept. For example, a candidate for a financial reporting analyst position may be asked about his or her knowledge of financial reporting rules, laws, and regulations, as well as financial reporting systems. Similarly, a staff accountant position may require knowledge of technical financial and/or managerial accounting – hence the need for earning a Certified Public and/or Managerial Accountant (i.e. CPA, CMA) designation.

Behavioral questions are designed to reveal how you would address or react to a given situation. For example, a candidate for a customer service position may be asked how he or she addressed an irate customer or perhaps a conflict with another company employee. Behavioral questions are used frequently, because employers want to better assess your people skills. Customer service and consulting opportunities incorporate behavioral interviews, because these jobs involve extensive customer/client contact. While internal and/or external conflicts are a normal part of business, your ability to successfully manage such situations is a key differentiator for potential employers. Behavioral questions allow a prospective employer to size you up for the job, while assessing your marketability for future opportunities.

Finally, the *"think on your feet" questions* are designed to catch a prospective job candidate off guard. The whole idea is to assess how quickly you can think about a question and provide a well-thought-out answer. For example, a hiring manager in the consulting industry once asked me, "If you could be any brand in the world, which brand would you be and why?" I knew this question had nothing to do with the job I wanted. However, the ability to think before you speak is a skill many often take for granted. This was a verbal test of how I could listen carefully, think quickly, and speak credibly.

Table 6 illustrates the three interview question categories as well as some sample questions for each category.

Table 6 – Categories of Common Interview Questions

Technical	Behavioral	"Think Fast"
How would you rate your MS Office skills?	What is your preference: work independently or collaboratively?	If you could be any brand in the world, what brand would you be?
Tell me about your account reconciliation experience	How do you manage work related conflicts and/or stress?	If you had a chance to go to the moon for free, would you go? If not, why not?

Of course, this table is by no means an exhaustive list of questions, which reveals the **21st practical concept to follow in the work life journey – always do your research to give yourself the best chance to successfully answer questions during the interview.** There are many resources available to help you prepare for interviews. Ask family members, friends or business colleagues for their help and advice. The Internet is also an invaluable resource for researching commonly asked interview questions. The library, as well as career centers at colleges, also can offer a wealth of resources for interview preparation.

Over the years, I have come to realize there is always someone who can do the job better, smarter and in perhaps in less time – just be glad you have not met this person. While this may be more comical than reality, you should always remember the impression you make today may be the only chance to keep your candidacy alive for the job going forward. As in the case of writing a resume, you may want to seek help in preparing for the phone or face-to-face interview.

The **22nd practical concept to remember in your work life journey – it is OK to be nervous during an interview – so long as the nerves do not prevent you from listening carefully and speaking credibly.** Actually, I would be more concerned if you were not nervous at all, since a lack of nerves tends to convey an image of over-confidence. Simple words of wisdom would suggest humility is always better than an overly zealous or over-confident demeanor and attitude.

Finally, the interview is also an opportunity for you to ask questions. Remember, just as the prospective employer is evaluating your background and strengths, you also can evaluate the prospective employer. Be inquisitive about the company, the job and the roles and responsibilities. Your ability to ask well-thought-out questions can help make a good impression.

The act of asking purposeful questions sends an important message to the prospective employer. It demonstrates you are thinking carefully about the next step in your work life journey. Table 7 presents some example questions to ask prospective employers. Remember, the questions you ask a prospective employer are also evaluated, so preparation is critical.

Table 7 – Sample Questions to Ask the Interviewer

What is the top priority for the position in the first 30 to 60 days?
What are your top goals and objectives for this role?
How do you see this position evolving in the future?
What do you like most about this organization?
How would you describe the ideal candidate for this role?

These questions are just the starting point for you to carefully evaluate the potential job opportunity. Again, just as a prospective employer asks questions about your background, you also have the right to carefully evaluate the prospective employer. The key is to think about the potential job opportunity with these questions/factors in mind:

How does the job opportunity relate to your inventory of personal attributes?

What are the roles and responsibilities of the position?

What is the reputation of the company and is it financially stable?

What are the organizational values, vision, and mission?

Is there any recent news about the company (if applicable)?

What is your impression of the executive management team?

What do you know about the products or services the company offers?

What customers or clients do business with the company (if available)?

Power of Non-Verbal Communication

Your ability to communicate your personal brand effectively with a well-written resume and the actual phone or face-to-face job interview is a key element of the job search process. However, you cannot underestimate the **23rd practical concept of the work life journey – the significant power of non-verbal communication.** Studies have shown an overwhelming majority (as much as 90% or more) of our normal everyday communication is non-verbal. Your facial expressions, eye contact, arm, and hand movements, as well as other forms of gestures like posture, handshakes, or physical spacing are forms of non-verbal communication.

It is not just what you say, but how you say it. Your non-verbal communication can be the difference between making a positive first impression versus being among the first eliminated from further consideration for the job. Given the importance of non-verbal communication, here are a few suggestions to keep in mind:

- *Dress for success* – appropriate attire is important, such as suits for men and women. Conservative colors (e.g., black, gray, or navy blue) are preferred over flashy or trendy looks. We typically first react to what we see followed by what we hear.
- A *firm handshake* reveals confidence and expresses interest in the interview and potential opportunity. A soft handshake typically expresses a timid or shy personality, lack of confidence and a strong sign of nervousness.
- *Eye contact* throughout the interview is essential. However, avoid staring at the interviewer. Rather, it is good to maintain eye contact long enough to demonstrate respect for the

interviewer, while expressing concentration on the question
being asked (so you can emphasize the ability to think before
you speak). Additionally, a healthy dose of eye contact also
sends a positive message you are fully engaged in the
interview discussion.

- *Avoid fidgeting* with anything (e.g., writing implement, coins,
  keys) or bouncing your knee up and down or tapping your
  feet on the floor. These are classic signs of uncontrollable and
  annoying nerves. Stay calm and keep your arms, hands, and
  feet still and relaxed. Mock interviews are an excellent way to
  practice your interviewing skills and understanding your non-
  verbal communication. You also can accomplish this by
  looking at yourself in the mirror and practicing your answers
  to common interview questions.

- *Avoid other signs of nerves*, potential over confidence, or
  disinterest, such as crossing your arms in front of your chest,
  which can suggest disinterest, conflict, or lack of
  understanding/agreement.

- *Be careful of your posture* – sit upright comfortably; avoid
  leaning back as you may look too casual; do not lean too far
  forward as if you are ready to invade the interviewer's space.

- *Listen carefully* – this is important for two reasons: it shows
  respect for the interviewer, and it will allow you to answer
  questions carefully and completely. The more you focus on
  the interviewer and listen carefully the less time you will have
  to show your nerves and feel helpless anxiety.

- *Finally, write correctly and effectively* – your personal brand is
  associated with everything you write (notes, memos, e-mails,
  formal letters, and reports). So, you owe it to yourself to
  make sure you write with proper grammar, punctuation, and
  style. Focus on reader benefits.

> **Personal Challenge:**
>
> How would you describe your non-verbal communication skills?
>
> What do others say about your non-verbal communication skills?
>
> How can improve your non-verbal communication skills?

Pre and Post Interview Checklists

A good practice for any interview – either over the phone or face-to-face – is to create and follow a pre-interview checklist. This checklist provides reassurance you have adequately prepared for the interview.

Table 8 – Pre-interview checklist

Activity/Task	Done	In-Process	Not Started
Research the organization	X		
Review the job description	X		
Research the interviewer		X	
Practice your personal branding message			X
Prepare for common interview questions		X	
Focus on being positive, thinking positive, and speaking confidently		X	
Dress for success		X	
Have interview logistics ready			X
Have an extra copy of your resume ready	X		

Of course, just as a pre-interview checklist helps you to prepare before the interview, a post-interview checklist ensures you follow-up the interview timely and successfully. Once again, you want to demonstrate professionalism and courtesy in everything you do regarding the interview.

— ◆ —

Table 9 – Post-Interview Checklist

Activity/Task	Done	In-Process	Not Started
Prepare "Thank You" email for the interviewer(s)			X
Provide follow-up information if requested			X

The active job search is a process designed to help you make a successful transition in your work life journey. Therefore, you owe it to yourself to do your homework and prepare to make the best possible impression. Remember, there is *no such thing as a second chance to make a first impression.*

Renewal

"I will prepare and someday my chance will come."
Abraham Lincoln

Stay Positive and Keep the Faith

Monday, February 2nd – Bob sits at the kitchen table with Mary talking about the past several weeks, since the layoff. So far, Bob has applied to 49 job opportunities he believes are in line with his inventory of personal attributes. However, Bob has had only one phone interview resulting from those job inquiries. Given market conditions, Bob knows he is lucky to have one interview.

As they drink coffee and snack on fresh-baked biscuits, Bob looks at Mary and smiles, yet his eyes show signs of deep despair. Mary quickly grabs Bob's hand and echoes her original words of encouragement, "Honey, don't worry, we will get through this together. We need to think positive and believe good things will happen."

Most people want the job search to be a sprint to the next step in the work life journey. Of course, you want to find the next job as quickly as possible. However, you must also prepare emotionally and psychologically for a marathon as opposed to a sprint. The reason is simple – you are not in control of recruiting and hiring activities at prospective employers. Therefore, your preparation is critical throughout the job search process.

Bob recognizes just how lucky he is to have such a loving and compassionate life-long partner in Mary. He knows how a layoff can weaken or sometimes even destroy a relationship. As they continue to talk about the job search, Mary continues to offer words of encouragement, "Honey, we cannot allow ourselves to take rejection personally. We need to stay positive and focused." Mary's words present the **24th practical concept in the work life journey – avoid taking rejections in the job search personally.** Remember, you cannot control the hiring process. You can only focus on your job search efforts.

Bob starts wondering if he made any mistakes during his interviews. "I wonder if I said the wrong things, or could have done something differently." Mary stops Bob before he can say anything further. "Honey, I am sure you said the right things; we just have to be patient and keep faith that a good opportunity will come our way soon."

Then, as if the world was listening to Bob and Mary talking, a news story appears on the kitchen television. The morning show is interviewing several people laid off across the United States. These real people find themselves under financial stress and trying to overcome the emotional and psychological impacts of the layoff.

One person, Chris, is particularly interesting to Bob and Mary. Chris talks about how life took on a new meaning after his layoff. For years, Chris thought a layoff would not impact him. Chris was the accounting manager for an organization with a solid reputation and history of strong financial performance. In fact, the company never laid off any people in its 57-year history. One day, Chris was called into a meeting, where his boss informed him his position in the company had been eliminated. Chris had no idea his job was in jeopardy. To compound matters, Chris recently purchased a brand-new condominium.

At the time of the interview, it had been several months, since Chris lost his job. Given his knowledge, skills and experience, Chris never imagined being in this position for such a long time. Yet, Chris maintains a positive outlook on life and fully understands a higher power is in full control of the world as we know it. There are too many factors we cannot control – like the economy, financial markets, and hiring decisions.

Therefore, we must learn to focus on those factors we can control or influence – our thoughts, dreams, hopes, beliefs, values, behavior, attitude, and faith. Suddenly, Bob realizes his situation is not unique. Rather, Bob is one of many hard-working people across the country to have experienced a drastic life-changing event – the layoff.

After watching the stories of other people impacted by a layoff, Bob and Mary look at the list of questions Bob recalls from the interviewers.

"Tell me about yourself."

"Why are you looking to work at this company?"

"What are you career goals?"

"What did you like most about your last job?"

"How can you add value in this role?"

Bob shares his thought process with Mary for answering those interview questions. In the end, they both believe his approach to answering the questions is good. Bob just needs to keep trying and staying positive, which is easier said than done. However, Bob is fortunate for having so many people support his efforts and offer words of encouragement, which keeps his spirits high as he continues to explore suitable job opportunities.

The conversation between Bob and Mary offers the **25th practical concept to remember in your work life journey – hope, faith, and trust are essential in the job search process.** Be thankful for your family, friends, and colleagues because they understand your situation. They are trying to help you overcome the daily emotional rollercoaster created by the layoff. "Today is a new day, the start of a new week – the start of new month – so let's stay positive and keep looking for the right opportunity," says Mary. Bob knows Mary is absolutely right. As the phone rings, Bob leaves the kitchen to continue the regular activities in his job search process.

A New Beginning

Tuesday, February 10th, 3:45 PM – Sally arrives for her 4 p.m. interview at ABC Consumer Products Company about 20 miles from her home. Sally is prepared for her interview. However, she is very nervous, and she needs to relax before going into the office. Since she arrives early, Sally plays "What a Wonderful Day" on a CD in her car stereo. The classic song makes her smile and always calms her down. She waits patiently in the lobby for Marylyn to greet her. Marylyn is the vice president of operations for the company and is looking to fill the customer service manager role due to the departure of the previous manager.

If anybody understands the criticality of quality customer service, Sally does. Marylyn begins the interview by giving Sally some background on the company as well as the customer service function, which she has managed for the past two years. During that time, Marylyn promoted a staff member to the manager position to alleviate some of her daily workload. However, a recent series of customer challenges, coupled with the departure of the previous manager, have made Marylyn's life extremely difficult. While the customer challenges have been successfully addressed, the need for a new manager remains a top priority.

"So Sally, what exactly was your role at your previous employer?" asks Marylyn. Sally immediately begins to explain her daily responsibilities in vivid detail, speaking about how she was the only customer service and billing resource in the company. Then, after some time, management decided to add one additional person to help Sally manage her workload more effectively. Marylyn quickly realizes, during the discussion, Sally is a confident person with a strong understanding of the customer service function.

However, Marylyn is concerned about Sally's minimal experience with customer relationship management systems, which is an essential part of the job. Nevertheless, Sally demonstrates she is a quick learner and has the aptitude and desire to expand her knowledge and abilities in the customer service arena. Marylyn is impressed with Sally and starts to discuss the managerial responsibilities of the job.

"Let's talk more about your responsibilities at your previous employer," said Marylyn. "Tell me about a situation where you had a conflict with a coworker and what you did to resolve the situation," Marylyn says. Once again, Sally is ready for such a question, as she remembers all the time she spent with Joe, the coffee shop owner.

Marylyn and Sally meet for about 40 minutes, during which time they both gain a good understanding of each other. Marylyn informs Sally a decision is expected as soon as possible. However, there are a few additional candidates in the mix, so any decision may not occur until the end of the following week at the earliest. "No problem," Sally says in a confident and cheerful voice. "I completely understand and look forward to the opportunity to continue our conversation, when you are ready."

***

Sally believes she may have found her new employer. While Sally is not overconfident, she just has a good feeling about this latest interview. However, only time will tell whether Marylyn thinks Sally is the right candidate for the job. Meanwhile, Sally heads back to the coffee shop to give Joe an update regarding her job search. For the past five weeks, Sally has met with Joe many times to continue her preparation for making a successful professional transition. The time and commitment are starting to give Sally hope for the future.

Wednesday, March 4th, 9:15 AM – Bob arrives early for his 9:30 a.m. interview for an accounting supervisor position at the Allied Manufacturing Company located about 30 minutes from Bob's home. Since Bob first applied for the job on Careerbuilder.com, he believes he has done his homework on the company and is ready for the interview.

Bob cannot help feeling nervous, so he takes a deep breath and whispers a small prayer for good luck. Then, just like he has done every day of his professional life, he looks at a photo of his family he keeps in his car and reminds himself about what matters most in his life. These thoughts and a single photo put Bob's mind at ease and give him confidence to do his best in the interview.

"Good morning, Bob. Did you find your way to the office OK?" asks Katie, the senior recruiter. As Bob and Katie get on the elevator, they continue their small talk on the way to Katie's office for the first of two interviews he will have this day. Katie starts the discussion by talking about the company and the opportunity for which Bob is interviewing. Katie recognizes Bob has a wealth of accounting and finance experience, but she wants to know more about Bob the person. "So, Bob, tell me about yourself," Katie says.

Bob takes a deep breath before responding. Soon he is walking Katie through a well-organized summary of his personal branding message, as well as future career interests. In all, Katie asks Bobs nine questions about his background, previous job, and future goals. Bobs answers each question with clarity and honesty. However, Bob's nerves do catch up with him on occasion, as he struggles to clear his throat and stop himself from twirling the pen in his hand. Remember, it is OK to be nervous, so long as you do not let the nervousness control your thought process and speaking ability. For the most part, Bob communicates credibly with Katie.

The time is 10:15 a.m. and Katie knows Bob's next interview is scheduled for 10:30 a.m. with Peter, the controller. So, Katie asks Bob, "Do you have any questions for me?" Once again, Bob takes a moment to collect his thoughts and asks some basic questions about her time with the company, the recruiting process, and the timeframe for making a hiring decision. Satisfied with Katie's responses, Bob thanks Katie for her time and says he looks forward to speaking to her again.

"Thank you so much for the opportunity to meet with you Bob. I really enjoyed our conversation," Katie says, smiling. "Now, I am going to walk you over to Peter's office for your last interview today." Katie introduces Bob to Peter and once again thanks Bob for his visit to company. Bob is immediately impressed with Peter's office, as it has an impressive view of the local skyline and nearby forest preserve. Equally impressive is the décor in the office, which displays a simple, elegant style – everything is neat and orderly.

As controller, Peter is a busy man. He quickly launches into the discussion, first giving Bob an overview of the accounting and financial reporting functions at the company. Peter speaks decisively without many words; Bob knows Peter is a no-nonsense member of the executive team. However, Peter also has a good sense of humor, so he breaks the ice a bit with some witty remarks about his role in the company. Peter then talks about how the accounting supervisor position is a newly created position due to recent staffing changes in the company.

The company is generally lean with only 50 employees at the headquarters location. However, the company has more than 400 employees at manufacturing plants across the United States and Canada. The accounting department was particularly short-staffed with only Peter, his administrative assistant Patty, and a junior accountant named Carlos. "The company is expecting to grow aggressively over the next three years. As such, there is a need to hire an experienced accountant who can effectively manage the daily accounting responsibilities for the entire company," says Peter with genuine enthusiasm.

"Bob, I see you have quite a bit of accounting experience, so tell me about your previous job and the role you played on a daily basis," asks Peter with keen interest in his eyes. Peter then asks whether Bob has any practical experience with tax analysis and compliance. Bob replies, "Yes, I actually prepared federal, state, and local tax returns for my previous employer, as well as managed the monthly tax provision process. We also worked with a consulting firm on specific tax matters including FIN 48 and FAS 109," Bob further explains.

"That's great Bob. We certainly need that kind of knowledge and experience in our company," Peter says. "Right now, it is pretty much me and Carlos, a junior accountant, which is why we are in the process of recruiting the right person for the job," Peter continues to explain. Peter and Bob meet for about 45 minutes, after which Peter also asks Bob if he has any questions. Bob asks specific questions about the position, the opportunity for advancement, and the immediate expectations for the selected candidate.

Based on Peter's responses, Bob asks one final question, "What is the next step in the recruiting process?" The follow-up question is, "How soon are you looking to make a hiring decision?" Satisfied with Peter's responses, Bob expresses his sincere thanks to Peter for his time and consideration, and says he looks forward to the opportunity to work with Peter.

Consider Another Industry or Vocation

...

In the aftermath of a layoff, keep the **26th practical concept in the work life journey in mind – the ability to demonstrate strong technical skills, coupled with a flexible approach to the job search process, may offer a unique opportunity or unplanned need to make a transition into a different industry.** For example, both Bob and Sally possess knowledge and skills they can transfer from one industry to another.

However, industry knowledge is also a critical success factor to remember, when contemplating an industry change. While the fundamentals of accounting and customer service remain the same, industry dynamics can vary greatly. In addition, there may be other factors to consider including regulatory dynamics and product versus service companies. Again, you need to do your homework when thinking about changing industries.

Sometimes another industry may offer the best chance to continue the work life journey. Remember, you cannot control economic conditions or competitive pressures, which often dictate recruiting and hiring trends in your current industry. This brings me to the **27th practical concept in the work life journey – the key for any successful industry transition is to fully understand and appreciate the challenges and potential risks behind making such transitions.** Figure 6 illustrates the spectrum of opportunities and challenges with industry and skills transitions.

Figure 6 – Industry and Skills Transition Grid

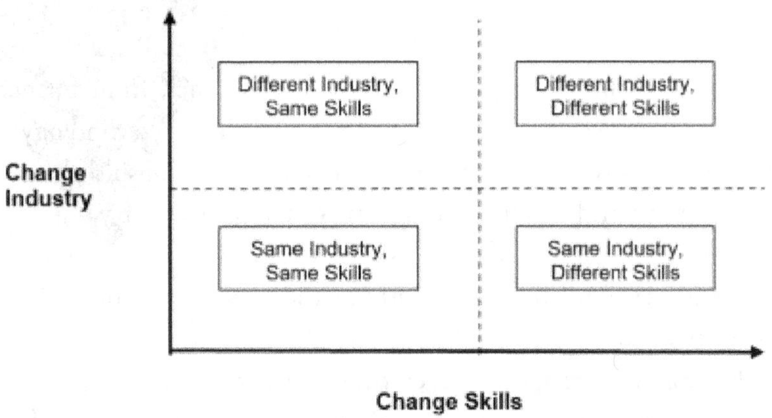

If you possess transferable knowledge and skills, you may want to consider new industries and companies in your work life journey. On the other hand, you can also consider acquiring new knowledge and skills through continuing education activities, certification programs or formal post-graduate level studies. Again, take time to reflect on your work life journey both before and after the layoff to fully assess your strengths and interests. The path of least resistance is maintaining your current skills and knowledge and either migrating to a different organization within the same industry or seeking a similar position in a different industry.

However, there are times when a more challenging course of action may offer the best alternative. I have often told friends and colleagues to remember there are other people who possess more knowledge, greater skills and have more experience – just be glad you have not met them yet! Therefore, assessing your inventory of personal attributes is a continuous process and is particularly critical after a layoff. As a result, you may find changing industries presents a genuine opportunity to acquire new knowledge and skills to successfully author the next chapter of your work life journey.

———◦———

In my case, I have changed industries several times, from financial services to management consulting to information technology to professional development training to management consulting again, and now the world of state government. While each industry transition required unique knowledge and skills, a critical common factor for each industry transition was a strong focus on exceptional client/customer service.

Early in my career, I was a member of the corporate tax department of a very large, global financial services company. Although I did not have an accounting degree or CPA license, the chief tax officer believed I had other talents that could add value to the department. Specifically, I had established strong relationships with personnel across the organization, which could allow me to gain better access to data and information necessary for several tax-related processes and activities (i.e., tax compliance and the preparation of corporate income tax returns).

Next, I joined the largest international accounting and management consulting organization in the world as a senior risk management consultant. I was hired by the partner of the business risk strategy consulting practice. He believed my diverse background and knowledge of business risk management could help establish an emerging consulting practice in the firm.

The next industry transition introduced me to the world of information technology as a strategic marketing professional. I still recall the interview with the president of the company, who instantly recognized we could collaborate on large sales opportunities across the United States. This job was one of the most challenging and exciting roles I have had in my work life journey.

From there, I found myself running my own business developing and delivering a variety of professional development training programs to corporate clients. I offered practical training programs on topics including dynamic communication, contemporary business etiquette, effective presentation skills and project management basics. Ironically, one of my last professional training projects as an entrepreneur involved multiple sessions regarding the impact of regulatory compliance (i.e., the Sarbanes-Oxley Act, section 404) on corporate information technology. These training sessions eventually led me back to the management consulting industry, where I assisted clients of all sizes across multiple industries with Sarbanes-Oxley compliance and business process improvement projects.

Today, I apply my practical knowledge, experience and expertise in state government, where I have applied my personal brand in various roles including deputy chief accountability officer, chief financial officer, and currently chief operating officer. I am living proof that work life transitions can indeed occur. However, preparation, commitment, and determination remain critical to developing and marketing your personal brand.

Such industry transitions are not without challenges. Therefore, research and preparation are essential to understanding and making successful industry transitions, which may also require you to acquire new skills and knowledge.

Take the Next Step

After a stressful and perhaps exhausting job search, you finally have a real job offer. Congratulations. So, what do you do now? Conventional thoughts suggest you should take the next step without hesitation. However, just like signing a contract, you should consider all aspects of the job offer – salary, benefits, and other rewards if applicable. Most people, including me in the early part of my work life journey, believe money is by far the most important aspect of any job offer. While I agree, money is a major part of the job offer, I also believe you should know and consider other benefits of value the job has to offer before accepting the job. For example, you might consider the following matters when evaluating a job offer:

- How much vacation time will you get?
- Does the job offer the opportunity to earn a bonus?
- What are the health benefits? And, are you and/or your family covered from day one?
- What is the policy on educational reimbursement if you want to pursue advanced studies?
- Does the job provide any retirement savings opportunities, like a 401k plan?

There are many things to think about when evaluating a job offer. The Internet is a valuable research tool for getting more information about evaluating and negotiating job offers. There is no blueprint for discussing compensation and/or benefits of a job offer. However, preparation is critical – just as it is for the job interview process. Remember, only you know what aspects of the job offer are most important to you. So, assess your unique situation and prioritize your needs and "nice to haves" as you evaluate the new job opportunity.

———◉———

So, now let's get to Bob, Sally, and Vince; how is their job search going?

Thursday, March 5th, 8 AM – After two months of working on odd jobs, Vince meets with Gary, a plant manager of a local steel-processing plant. While Vince's skills were more on the assembly side of manufacturing, he is a quick study and wants to pursue other production-oriented opportunities to diversify his manufacturing experience. Gary is looking for a reliable, hard-working person to fill the need for a new steel processor role for the first or third shift. Vince is eager to learn more about the company and its local plant operations.

During their discussion, Vince points out some ideas of how to improve quality and production, which impresses Gary. After a 45-minute discussion and tour of the plant facility, Gary offers Vince the job on the spot. Vince is elated and cannot wait to start. After stopping at the central office to complete the job-related paperwork, Vince is told he should report for work on Friday morning 7:30 a.m. sharp for orientation.

Vince heads home for the day and immediately calls his wife and his friends to share the good news. They all agree to meet at the local pub for dinner, drinks and some quality time playing pool.

Monday, March 9th, 10 AM – Nine weeks after the layoff, and five weeks since her interview with Marylyn, Sally receives a phone call from Marylyn. And, the news for Sally is positive. After a lengthy search, Marylyn decides to offer Sally the job as customer service manager, starting Monday, March 16th. Marylyn also encourages Sally to finish her college degree while working for the company. The company has a policy that allows employees to be eligible for tuition reimbursement after one year of employment.

Sally is overjoyed with the news and cannot wait to start her new job with a new employer. She calls Joe to tell him the good news as well. "That's wonderful Sally, congratulations," says an equally jubilant Joe. "The next time you visit the coffee shop, we are going to celebrate," Joe shouts with excitement.

When Ashley arrives home from another long day at high school, she is greeted at the door by her best friend – her mom. Sally has already made plans for the evening; she and Ashley are going out for dinner to celebrate the good news. Sally and Ashley grab their coats and head to the local Italian restaurant. "Mom, I am so happy for you – for both of us," says a thrilled Ashley as she wipes away tears of joy.

Wednesday, April 8th, 9 AM –13 weeks after being laid off, and five weeks since the interview with Peter, Bob receives a call from Katie. "Hi Bob. I know you are probably wondering where we are in the recruiting process, so I wanted to give you a call and give you some good news," Katie says. "First, thank you again for your patience during our extensive recruiting process. I want you to know you made quite an impression on Peter," continues Katie. "We are very interested in you joining our team, and therefore would like to extend you an offer of employment for the accounting supervisor position reporting directly to Peter, the vice president and controller," says Katie.

Bob's reactions are relief and excitement at the same time. Given the current economic conditions, Bob had braced himself for a potentially lengthy job search. However, faith and hope were on Bob's side sooner than he ever anticipated. Katie explains the details of the job offer to Bob and says he will receive the official offer of employment and related material via express mail within two days. Bob is absolutely elated and cannot wait to tell Mary and their children, who were all so supportive during what was a challenging time for the entire family.

Author the Next Chapter

The layoff situation is emotionally, psychologically, socially, and financially stressful. Remember, you have no control over when the next step in the work life or professional journey will take place. Therefore, you should only focus on areas you can either control or influence:

- Understand the emotional and psychological migration.
- Have a focused and positive attitude.
- Be confident and have faith.
- Seek guidance from your mentors and role models.
- Network with family, friends, and colleagues.
- Create an inventory of personal attributes.
- Write a well-written resume.
- Understand the C.H.A.R.M. factor.
- Prepare a handbill document.
- Create a personal business card.
- Prepare for interviews.

After a layoff, your focus is on finding the next full-time job. However, an excellent alternative to traditional salaried jobs is to embrace the **28th practical concept in the work life journey – consider temporary or contract-based opportunities as an effective bridge between the layoff and the next permanent job.**

Temporary or contract employment offers you an opportunity to prove your value to the employer, which may lead to a permanent job. Temporary work can also provide a variety of opportunities with different companies. You may encounter different roles and responsibilities within those companies. Keep in mind temporary opportunities can also expand your network and give you exposure to different industries.

———◉———

During my daily commute to work via the train, I often meet different people. I recall a conversation with Pete, an information technology (IT) professional. Pete was laid off from his previous job as an IT manager for a large financial services company. After being laid off, Pete became a temporary contract professional. He told me his skills were transferable to other industries, since IT was a critical need for all organizations.

One day, Pete interviewed for a contract IT opportunity for a large financial services/banking organization. Although Pete had a lot of competition for the work, he was the candidate selected. Over the next several months, Pete helped the company complete a major application integration project. Pete's contributions did not go unnoticed, as the senior vice president of technology approached Pete about a permanent role in the IT department.

After a lengthy interview process, Pete was given an offer to join the company as vice president. He accepted the offer. Pete's time as a contract worker had a direct impact on the next chapter in his work life journey. I am not suggesting every temporary or contract-based opportunity can lead to a permanent job. However, the temporary positions provide the opportunity to continue the work life journey in the aftermath of a layoff.

———◉———

For Bob, Sally and Vince, the next steps in their respective work life journeys came relatively quickly. However, not all work life transitions occur with such expediency. Rather, you should keep in mind the **29th practical concept in the work life journey – set realistic and attainable goals and objectives.** For example, you may want to make

10-15 calls per day or try to meet two or three new people per day. People often forget finding a job is often a full-time job itself. So, it helps to be organized and spend your time wisely. Remember, the transition to the next destination in the work life journey is not a sprint – be ready for a marathon.

In addition, it is wise to acknowledge the **30th practical concept in the work life journey – be patient and diligent in your job search.** Remember, you cannot control who will invite you for an interview much less give you an offer of employment. However, a positive approach, a healthy dose of discipline and a strong commitment to change go a long way toward helping you get back on the path to finding the next step in the work life journey. For Bob, Sally, and Vince, the hiring decisions were not something they could control. However, faith, hope, and trust were fully within their control.

Focus on Professional Development

Once you succeed in creating a work life transition, focus on managing your career. You should commit to learning new skills and acquiring more knowledge. In addition, you should take on new responsibilities and increase your network of contacts. Remember to pursue ways to demonstrate your knowledge and talents, which can ultimately enhance your overall value and marketability. This is the essence of the **31st practical concept in the work life journey – explore training programs or formal academic classes to reinforce current knowledge and abilities, while acquiring new skills in the process.**

You are the only one in control of your actions, choices, and decisions. Therefore, you need to develop a disciplined approach in your work life journey. The rewards are there for those willing to play by the rules, take responsibility for their own actions and understand the power of communication and relationship building.

"An investment in knowledge always pays the best interest."
Benjamin Franklin

Enhance Professional Development/ Networking

The work life journey inevitably involves many decisions and choices. While the journey can sometimes present daunting challenges, you can take some comfort in knowing there are many resources available at your disposal to help you overcome those challenges. Your network of contacts, coupled with the wealth of information available to you, offers the opportunity to successfully navigate the often-turbulent waters of the global workplace. In the end, you cannot control the dynamics of the global economy. Rather, you need to focus on your ability to learn and adapt to a rapidly changing business world filled with peaks and valleys.

Table 10 presents a sample of additional resources to gain valuable knowledge and information regarding the pursuit of successful transitions in the work life journey.

Table 10 – Additional Resources for Transition

Internet – uploading your resumes, networking, communicating with others	LinkedIn.com Indeed.com ZipRecruiter.com
Local events and places – for learning industry and occupational information	Job Fairs Trade Shows Professional Associations
People – for career advancement and management	Mentors and role models Career coaches/advisors

Prelude to Another Opportunity

The layoff is a life changing event, which creates a myriad of emotional, psychological, and financial challenges. However, the layoff also provides the opportunity for a new beginning, which may offer the chance to redirect your energy toward doing something new or different. Of course, life after a layoff requires greater focus, stronger discipline, and an open mind to identify and explore new opportunities to continue the work life journey.

However, never lose focus of this one fact: *only you are the maestro of your career*. No employer, career coach, career advisor or recruiter can decide your work life fate. In other words, no one else is going to manage your career – it's up to you.

Career coaches, recruiters and employers can present suggestions, ideas and sometimes opportunities you can evaluate. Some of these opportunities may present new challenges, which may offer greater success and personal rewards. However, such success and reward may not be easy to recognize. Again, you need to exercise caution and be patient to assess the opportunities that come your way in the work life journey. While you cannot control what job will be offered to you, or when or by whom, you decide whether the job is worth pursuing.

Above all, remember you are not alone in the process of overcoming a layoff. Talk to family, friends and colleagues for advice and help. There is also a wealth of information available for you to research, study and apply toward the continuation of your work life journey. While it may take time to fully overcome the emptiness of a layoff, the time and effort dedicated to looking beyond the layoff can revitalize and illuminate the path to finding work life fulfillment.

The practical concepts in this book are designed to stimulate thought, which hopefully will translate into meaningful actions toward achieving the next step in your work life journey. I encourage you to work diligently on developing your personal brand with the confidence, discipline, and attitude necessary to make a measurable difference, both personally and professionally. Remember, *learn from the past, embrace the present and plan for the future*. I strongly believe good things happen to good people.

I wish you much success in your work life journey today, tomorrow, and always.

Appendix – Summary of Practical Concepts

1. Understand the emotional and psychological migration
2. Always maintain good relations with everyone
3. Maintain a positive mental attitude
4. Volunteer to help others or worthy causes
5. Understand the CDA principle
6. Find a trustworthy mentor
7. Think about your role models
8. Establish a consistent schedule or routine
9. Identify and understand your inventory of personal attributes
10. Develop your personal branding message
11. Prepare a well-written and action-oriented resume
12. Identify resources to help you prepare the resume
13. Develop a disciplined approach to continuous professional development
14. Tell everyone you know about your layoff
15. Create a list of everyone you know
16. Identify the primary and secondary list of contacts
17. Self-discipline – stay in touch with your network of contacts
18. Understand your "C.H.A.R.M." factor
19. No second chance to make a good first impression
20. Prepare for the three categories of interview questions: technical, behavioral, and "think on your feet questions"
21. Always do your research before the interview
22. It is OK to be nervous during an interview
23. The significant power of non-verbal communication
24. Avoid taking rejections in the job search personally

25. Hope, faith, and trust are essential in the job search process
26. Consider a transition into different industry
27. Understand the risks and challenges of making transitions into different industries
28. Consider temporary or contract-based opportunities
29. Set realistic goals and objectives
30. Be patient and diligent in your job search
31. Explore training programs and/or formal classes to reinforce existing abilities, while acquiring new skills

About the Author

Sanjay Patel is an advisor, consultant, and speaker with over two decades of professional experience spanning multiple industries and business functions. He has made successful career transitions into the public, private, not-for-profit and government sectors of the economy. Sanjay also has owned and operated his own professional development training practice, serving clients across the United States. He is a recognized speaker at national conferences, as well as a graduate level instructor. Having experienced a layoff twice, Sanjay has applied the practical concepts in this book to overcome the challenges and adversity resulting from those layoffs. Sanjay holds an MS in Communication, Managerial Program from Northwestern University and MBA and BS degrees from DePaul University. He currently resides in Round Lake, IL., with his wife and three children.